HOW CAN YOU HELP?

Creative Volunteer Projects
for Kids Who Care

Written by Linda Schwartz • Illustrated by Bev Armstrong

The Learning Works

Type Design and Editorial Production: Kimberley A. Clark

The Learning Works, Inc.
P.O. Box 6187
Santa Barbara, California 93160

Library of Congress Catalog Number: 93-0862-12
ISBN 0-88160-213-2

Printed in the United States of America. Current Printing (last digit): 10 9 8 7 6 5 4 3 2 1

Dedication

*This book is dedicated to
Bobbe Dartanner, Carol Nelson, and Phyllis Amerikaner,
friends who understand the true meaning
of giving and of helping others,
to my sons Stephen and Michael,
and to children everywhere
who, by reaching out to others,
have the power to make a difference.*

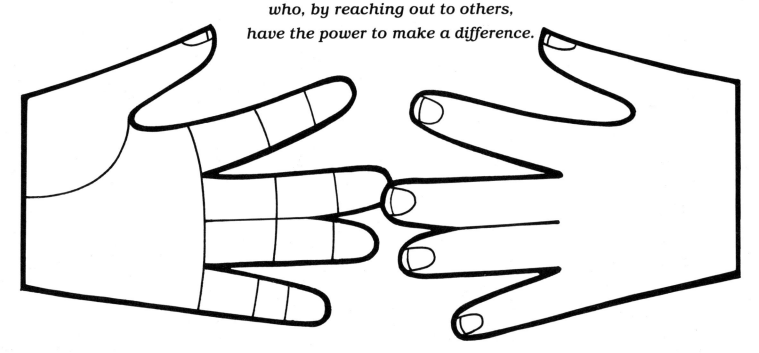

Acknowledgments

Sincere thanks to the following people for their expertise and contributions to **How Can You Help?**

Beverly Armstrong

Rae Aronoff

Dwight Barnett, Staff Forester, Tennessee Division of Forestry

Barbara Barton, President, Young at Heart

Kimberley Clark

Patty Hall

Kathy Lancaster, President, Nordhoff High School Booster Club

A. Michael Marzolla, Youth Development Advisor, 4-H

Candyce Norvell

Jim Palmer, Orange County Rescue Mission

Jan Roberta, Associate Executive Director, Girls Incorporated

Angela Antenore Sponder

Gabrielle Vidal

Ethyl Zivatofsky, Director, Jewish Family Service

Special thanks to the following "kids who care" for sharing their experiences. Hopefully, their stories will inspire you to create your own special projects and ways to get involved in helping others.

Jonathan Akchin	Jeff Wheeler
Sacha Bice	Matt Wheeler
Katy McKean	Stephanie Wolf
Billy Peevey	Stephen Wright
Melissa Poe	Aaron Wright
Grady Wheeler	Dustin Wright

Contents

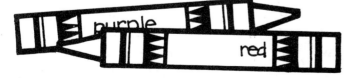

Contents
(continued)

Contents
(continued)

Contents
(continued)

Contents
(continued)

A Note to Kids

How Can You Help? is an idea book for kids, like you, who want to help others. Many times you and members of your scout troop, youth group, class at school, or family want to do something to help others but don't know how or where to start. This book helps by giving you lots of suggestions of things you can do to help children, the elderly, people in need, animals, your community, and your environment.

Pick a project that interests you and that you feel comfortable doing. Be creative. Add your own ideas and come up with other ways to accomplish the project—whether it's planting a tree in your neighborhood or helping to serve food at a shelter.

By helping others, you will also be helping yourself. When you volunteer, you

- meet new people and develop new friendships;

- expand your skills, knowledge, and interests;

- provide fun for those you help as well as for yourself; and

- feel good about yourself.

Most of all, enjoy yourself! Get your friends and family to help and make these projects a team effort. Good luck and have fun!

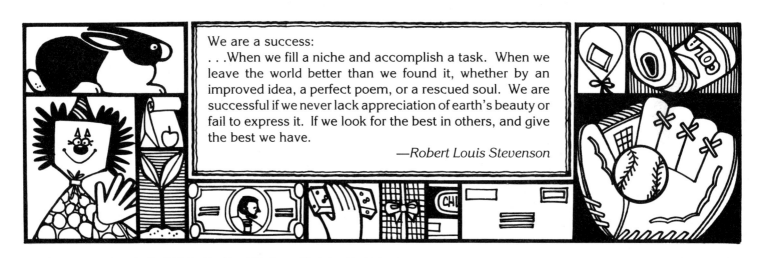

We are a success:
. . .When we fill a niche and accomplish a task. When we leave the world better than we found it, whether by an improved idea, a perfect poem, or a rescued soul. We are successful if we never lack appreciation of earth's beauty or fail to express it. If we look for the best in others, and give the best we have.

—Robert Louis Stevenson

How to Request Information

Volunteer organizations are working in your community, state, and country to help others. The names and addresses of some of these organizations are listed at the end of each section. Upon request, many of them will send you information about their programs and will tell you how you can get involved. When you write to these organizations, remember to do these four things:

1. Include your name and a complete return address so that the organization will know where to send the information you have requested.

2. Enclose two first-class stamps with your request. Many of these organizations have limited budgets. The stamps you enclose will be used as postage for the information they send to you. Attach the stamps to your letter with a paper clip so they don't get lost or overlooked.

3. Be patient. Many of these organizations are understaffed, and the members of their staffs have many other jobs to do. Expect to wait three to six weeks for a reply.

4. Make the most of any information you receive. Share it with your classmates, friends, and family members.

Questions to Ask

If you are planning to do volunteer work at a facility such as an animal shelter, a pre-school, a hospital, or a nursing home, it is a good idea to be prepared and organized before you begin. Here are some questions you might want to ask a responsible adult at the facility where you plan to donate your time. Ask other questions you have pertaining to your specific areas of interest.

- Do I need any experience for this task?

- Does your organization provide a special training or orientation program for volunteers?

- Do I need written permission from my parents?

- Is there a minimum commitment of service required per week or month?

- Will I work alone or in a group with other volunteers?

- What hours will I work?

- To whom do I report?

- What will my specific duties be on the job?

- What is the appropriate dress for the work I will be doing?

- Are there any special instructions I need to have?

Kids Who Care

A young leukemia patient in Mississippi who finished his treatment and got to go home didn't forget the kids who were still in the hospital. He visited them every week and took them to the zoo or to the movies when the doctors gave him permission.

Write letters to government leaders expressing your views. Here's an example of a letter one boy wrote to a U.S. Senator: "One of my major concerns is plastic waste and pollution in California and everywhere.... One way you could help is to educate more people about our situation and help pass laws about pollution...."

Two sisters in Texas started helping out at a food bank when they were only five and eight years old. They worked with their parents, packaging food for people in need. You're never too young to start helping others.

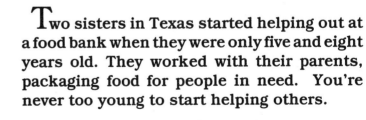

Kids Who Care
(continued)

A group of fourth graders in Massachusetts noticed that a creek where they played was so polluted that the frogs that lived near the creek were dying. They cleaned up all the trash around the stream, wrote a 36-page report called "Let the Frogs Leap Again," and even performed first aid on frogs that had been cut by broken glass. They received a Presidential Award for Excellence.

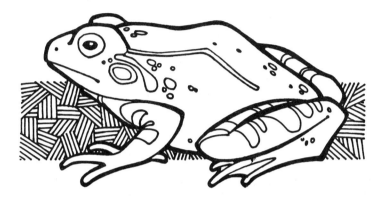

A class of fifth graders in New Jersey started an organization called Kids Against Pollution (KAP) to help the environment. KAP now has more than 150 chapters in 30 countries around the world. KAP members start community recycling programs, plant trees, protest the use of materials that can harm the environment, and help in many other ways.

One concerned girl shows she cares by recording messages about helping animals on her telephone answering machine. She changes the message every couple of weeks and includes the telephone number of an organization that helps animals in case her friends want to get involved.

Helping Children

Things To Think About

Volunteer your time to help children. There are many ways you can get involved. You might work directly with kids in a nursery school, in a kindergarten class, at a child-care center, in an after-school program, at a shelter for the homeless, in a pediatric wing of a hospital, or in other places where young children are receiving care.

Even if you are not old enough to work with kids in a hospital or other facility, there are many ways for you to help. This section suggests ideas for raising money to donate to organizations that help kids, ways to volunteer your time to worthy children's causes, and things you can do to make a difference in the life of a child.

It is one of the beautiful compensations of this life that no one can sincerely try to help another without helping himself.
—*Charles Dudley Warner*

Tape a Book

Grab a tape recorder, a blank cassette tape, and a favorite picture book you have out-grown. Here's your chance to create a read-along tape for a youngster who is sick or to give as a gift to a child for a special occasion.

Start by selecting a picture book you no longer read. Find a quiet place and time to tape so you won't be interrupted. Be sure to include a dedication to the child and to read the story slowly and clearly as you record it. Put a lot of expression in your voice as you read to make the story interesting and lively. Include the book as part of your gift so that the child can follow along as he or she listens to the tape. You will need a signal to let the child know when to turn each page, especially if the book is for a young child who can't read. Here are some ideas for creative signals you can use:

- ring a bell

- clang two pot lids together

- tap a spoon on the rim of a glass

- play a few notes on a piano or other musical instrument

At the beginning of the tape, explain to the listener that he or she should turn the page upon hearing that sound.

Teach a Skill

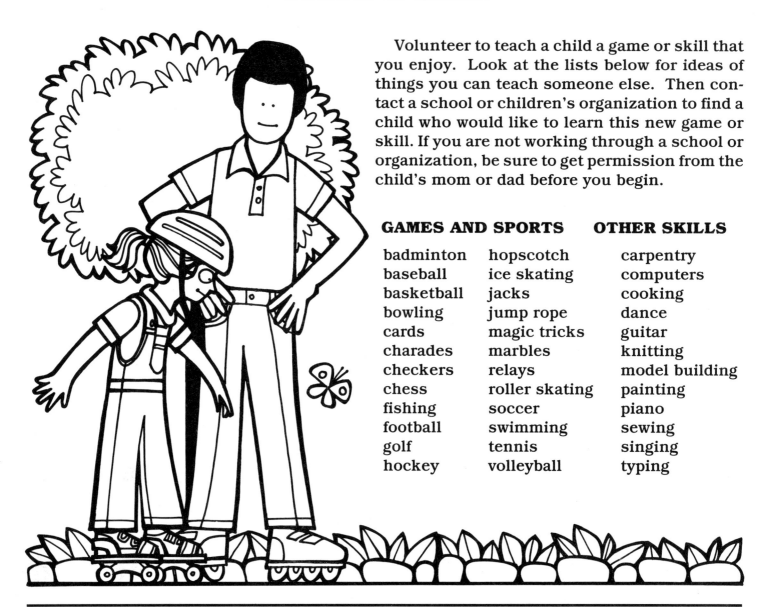

Volunteer to teach a child a game or skill that you enjoy. Look at the lists below for ideas of things you can teach someone else. Then contact a school or children's organization to find a child who would like to learn this new game or skill. If you are not working through a school or organization, be sure to get permission from the child's mom or dad before you begin.

GAMES AND SPORTS

badminton	hopscotch
baseball	ice skating
basketball	jacks
bowling	jump rope
cards	magic tricks
charades	marbles
checkers	relays
chess	roller skating
fishing	soccer
football	swimming
golf	tennis
hockey	volleyball

OTHER SKILLS

carpentry
computers
cooking
dance
guitar
knitting
model building
painting
piano
sewing
singing
typing

Produce a Puppet Show

A great way to entertain children is to put on a puppet show. Puppets can be used to read a book to a young child, to teach a song, or to "interview" a child about his or her interests. You can also do puppet shows for a group of kids at a shelter for the homeless, at your local library, or for a preschool or special education class in your community.

On a larger scale, puppets can be used to produce a show to raise money for a favorite children's charity or cause. Get together with a group of friends and spend an afternoon creating a short skit and making paper bag puppets for the main characters in your play. Directions for making the puppets are found on pages 20 and 21. Make a puppet stage for your production (page 22) and write a script for your puppet play.

After you've had several rehearsals, you'll be ready to perform! Design a flyer to announce the date, time, and location of your production. Be sure to mention which charity the show will benefit. Pass out your flyers to family, friends, classmates, relatives, and neighbors. Then, make tickets out of construction paper.

Sell your tickets in advance and at the door. Be sure to tell everyone that the money they pay to see your show will be given to the children's organization you have chosen. You might want to mention why you selected this particular charity and explain what this organization does.

Lights, camera, action! Let the show begin!

Make Paper Bag Puppets

Turn a paper bag into a puppet for your show. Rewrite a popular fairy tale, and make a puppet of the main character for your play. Here are instructions for how to make a head for your paper bag puppet.

WHAT YOU NEED TO MAKE THE HEAD AND BODY

- a paper lunch or grocery bag
- a piece of cloth about two feet square
- some newspapers
- a long cardboard tube
- two pieces of cardboard about six inches square
- a thin dowel about 15 inches long
- a pair of scissors
- glue
- masking tape
- stapler and staples
- crayons or felt-tipped pens
- odds and ends such as feathers, paper and fabric scraps, paper plates and cups, sticks, and yarn

WHAT YOU DO TO MAKE THE HEAD

1. Stuff the bag with newspapers.

2. Push one end of the cardboard tube into the middle of the newspapers, leaving part of the tube extended through the bag's opening to form the neck.

3. Squeeze the bag around the tube, and use masking tape to attach it securely.

4. With crayons or marking pens, draw a face on the bag.

5. Use some of your odds and ends to add a beak, a nose, ears, horns, hair, or fur.

Make Paper Bag Puppets
(continued)

After you have finished making the head, you are ready to make the body of your paper bag puppet.

WHAT YOU DO TO MAKE THE BODY

1. Fold the cloth in half.

2. With the scissors, cut a one-inch slit in the center of the fold for the tube, as shown.

3. Make cardboard hands for your puppet.

4. Staple or glue the hands inside the folded cloth.

5. Put the tube, or neck portion, of the puppet's head through the slit in the cloth.

6. Tape the edge of the cloth around the puppet's neck to hold it in place.

7. Tape the dowel to one of your puppet's hands.

To move your puppet, hold the tube in one hand and the dowel in the other, as shown.

Make a Puppet Stage

Now that you have finished making your puppet, you are ready to construct a stage for your show. Here are some fun ideas for your puppet stage.

A table turned on its side

A table top

A card table or piece of cloth across a doorway

A big box with a hole in it

A window

A broomstick and blanket between two chairs

Donate Reusable Toys

Look through your closet and check your shelves to find toys and games you have outgrown and no longer play with or use. Instead of throwing these toys and games away, clean and/or repair them, and donate them to a child-care center, a homeless shelter, a church or synagogue, or a school in your community.

Write a Book

Write and illustrate a book for a child in a hospital, homeless shelter, or kindergarten class. Your book can be a fairy tale, an adventure, a mystery, an animal story, a comic book, or whatever you think a younger child might enjoy reading. If the child is too young to read alone, an adult can read your book to him or her.

WHAT YOU NEED

- scratch paper
- pencil and pen
- colored pencils, crayons, or felt-tipped pens
- white art paper
- colored construction paper
- stapler and staples
- masking tape

"An adventure awaits!" announced Alvin.
"All aardvarks are assembling at Adelaide.
Anchors aweigh!"

Write a Book
(continued)

WHAT YOU DO

1. Use scratch paper to make a rough draft showing where your pictures will appear and where the text will be placed on each page.

2. When you have checked your rough draft for spelling errors, copy it onto white art paper. Write only one or two sentences on each page. Print in large, easy-to-read letters.

3. Illustrate each page using colored pencils, crayons, or felt-tipped pens.

4. Decorate a cover for your book using colored construction paper. Add a title page with your name as author and illustrator.

5. Staple your book and bind it with tape.

If possible, read the book you created to a child and let him or her keep it as a gift from you. Some hospitals and children's facilities have age restrictions for visitors. If you can't meet a child in person, include a stamped, self-addressed postcard so the child who receives your book can write a note to you, the author!

ALVIN AARDVARK'S AUSTRALIAN ADVENTURE
by Angela Chavez

Tutor a Child

Volunteer your time to tutor a child after school or on weekends. Contact schools, shelters, hospitals, or community organizations that reach out to children. Find a boy or girl who would benefit from an hour or two a week working with you in an area in which he or she needs help.

IDEAS FOR TUTORING

art
English
foreign language
geography
grammar
history
mathematics
music
phonics
physical education
reading
science
social studies
spelling
vocabulary
writing

Collect Change for Kids

Find a large plastic container and reuse it as a change bank. Collect spare change from your pockets and wallet each day. Ask family members and friends to add to your change collection. When the container is full, roll the money into change wrappers (available at most banks). Then take your wrapped change back to the bank and ask the teller to give you paper currency in exchange.

Here are some ideas for ways you can help younger children with the money you have collected:

Fun Things to Do with Children

- take them to a movie or sporting event
- do face paintings
- plan a picnic
- throw a party
- fly kites
- go to the zoo
- visit a museum

Things to Buy for Children

- blankets
- books
- cassette tapes
- clothing
- food
- games
- models
- school supplies
- stuffed animals
- toys

Plan a Read-a-Thon

One way to raise money for a children's organization is to schedule a read-a-thon. The basic idea behind a read-a-thon is to see how many books you can read in a specified period of time, such as a month. Before beginning, ask your family, friends, teachers, and neighbors to sign up as sponsors. These sponsors pledge a set amount of money for each book you read during the read-a-thon month. Let your sponsors know that the money they pledge is going to an organization that helps children.

Read-a-Thon Sign-Up Sheet

Name: _____

Money will be donated to: _____

I plan to read five books:

title	date completed

sponsor's name	amount pledged per book	total pledged

Plan a Read-a-Thon
(continued)

A read-a-thon can be done on a larger scale with a scout troop, your class at school, a religious youth group, or a group of your friends willing to volunteer time to help other kids. You will need the help and support of adults if you choose to do this project on a larger scale because it will take a lot of time, effort, and planning.

Ribbons or bookmarks can be presented to all kids who participate in the read-a-thon. Special awards, such as gift certificates from a local bookstore, can be given to those who read a specific number of books or raise the most money through pledges.

Here are a few ideas for other events. Use your imagination, and see how many more you can create.

- bike-a-thon
- dance-a-thon
- jog-a-thon
- skate-a-thon
- swim-a-thon
- walk-a-thon

Be an Aide

Volunteer your services to an organization or facility devoted to kids, such as a nursery school, a child-care or after-school center, a Girls' and Boys' Club, a youth group, or a local chapter of one of the organizations listed on pages 35 and 36. Here are some ways you may be able to help:

file papers	*type letters and memos*	*answer telephones*
use a copy machine	*stuff envelopes*	*help with a fund-raising event*
pass out supplies to kids	*work with an individual child*	*supervise a small group of kids*

Create a Kids' Club

Many young people have special interests but no way to pursue them. Why not organize a special-interest club for younger kids at your school? Start by getting together with your friends to brainstorm possibilities. Check with younger kids to find out about their needs and interests. Perhaps your club could meet during lunch recess or after school. (If your club will be meeting at school, be sure to check with your teachers and/or principal to get permission.)

Things to Think About

- Where will we meet?
- How often will we meet?
- Will we have rules and club officers?
- What will be our purpose?
- How many kids can we accommodate?

Many projects initiated during your club meetings can be completed by the kids at home. Use your meeting times to motivate the kids and to give them a chance to share their special interests with one another.

Ideas for Special-Interest Kids' Clubs

- art
- astronomy
- baseball cards
- books
- chess
- computers
- dance
- inventions
- music
- nature
- pets
- photography
- sports
- stamps

Make Kits for Kids

Make a school kit for a child. Look around your apartment or house for a box that is large enough to hold school supplies. Decorate the outside of the box. One idea is to cover the box with the Sunday comics after your family has read them. Another idea is to decorate the box around a theme you think a child would like. Here are some ideas for themes:

- School Days
- Collage of Cars
- Monster Mash
- Sports Galore
- Animals on Parade
- Space Spectacular

After your box is decorated, fill it with school supplies. Here are some items you might want to include:

- construction paper
- spiral note pad
- scissors
- felt-tipped pens
- pencils
- erasers
- a box of crayons
- a ruler

Add a greeting card to put inside your box!

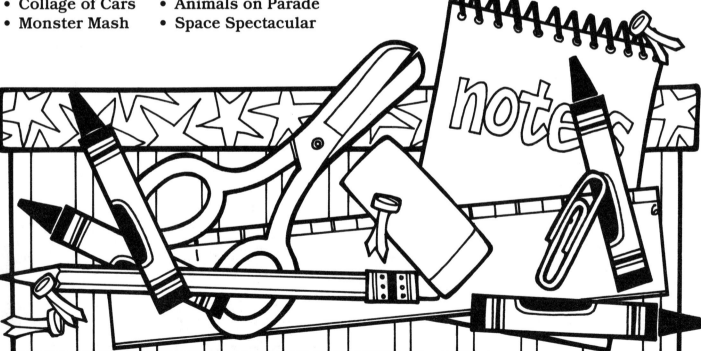

Help Save a Life

One of the most important ways you can help other children is by attending a training course in cardiopulmonary resuscitation or CPR. The skills you learn in a CPR training class can make the difference between life and death for a sibling, for a youngster you are baby-sitting, or for a child in an emergency situation. The American Red Cross provides classes in infant and child CPR. These classes teach you how to recognize and care for breathing and cardiac emergencies in infants and children. The classes also provide information on how injuries can be prevented.

The Amercian Red Cross offers a class called Basic Aid Training, designed for kids ages 8 to 10. The course introduces you to first aid procedures. Basic Aid Training includes information on choking, water safety and rescue, bicycle and car safety, and avoiding drugs and other harmful substances.

Check your telephone directory for the phone number of the local chapter of the American Red Cross. By signing up and taking the CPR class, you will be preparing yourself to save a child's life in an emergency.

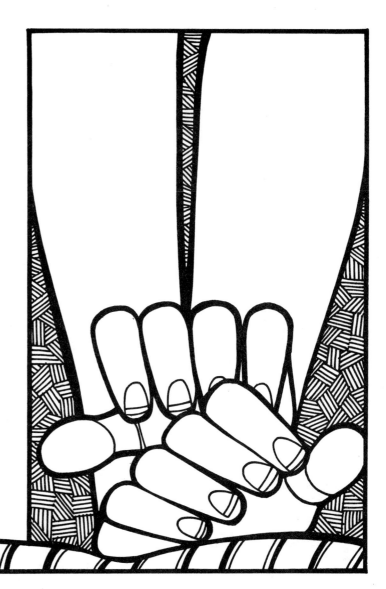

Kids Who Care

Aaron Wright is 11 years old and is in the sixth grade in Irvine, California.

He and his brothers Dustin, 14, and Stephen, 10, have lots of experience helping kids—their mother used to run a day-care center. Aaron played soccer with the kids, helped them make forts, and served them lunch. One of the kids, Kyle, has become Aaron's friend, even though Kyle is only four years old. Aaron and Kyle like to play video games together. One of the things Aaron has learned from helping out with younger kids is that your friends don't have to be the same age you are.

Aaron's school also has a "buddy" program that pairs older kids like Aaron with younger kids. Aaron's "buddy" is a second grader. One of the things they do together is draw pictures, and Aaron helps his "buddy" whenever he needs it.

The Nordhoff High School Booster Club in Ojai, California, is an organization that encourages kids to help kids in their own school. The club put on a wild and crazy fund-raising event called Plop-O-Rama! They divided the football field into 5,000 squares and "sold" each square for $5. Buyers got a "Land Lot Deed" identifying their square. Then, on an appointed day and time, three cows were released onto the field. The owner of the first square to be "plopped" on received $250. The second plop was good for $500, and the third plop earned that deed holder $1,000.

Each club, activity group, or class that sold squares got to keep $1 for each square they sold. The rest of the money went into the Booster Club's budget which is used to help Nordhoff High students in many different ways. One student at the school injured his leg seriously and couldn't afford to go to the doctor. When his friends told the Booster Club about the situation, club members paid for the student's medical care. To show his appreciation, the student now helps the Booster Club.

Organizations that Help Children

Here are the names and addresses of several organizations that benefit children. You can find the names of others by checking in your local library.

American Cancer Society
777 3rd Avenue
New York, NY 10017

American National Red Cross
17th and D Streets, N.W.
Washington, D.C. 20006

Big Brothers/Big Sisters of America
117 South 17th Street, Suite 1200
Philadelphia, PA 19103

Boys' and Girls' Clubs of America
771 First Avenue
New York, NY 10017

Boy Scouts of America
1325 W. Walnut Hill Lane
P.O. Box 152079
Irving, TX 75015–2079

Camp Fire Boys and Girls
4601 Madison Avenue
Kansas City, MO 64112–1278

Child Find of America, Inc.
7 Innis Avenue
P.O. Box 277
New Paltz, NY 12561–0277

Child Welfare League of America
440 First Street NW, Suite 310
Washington, D.C. 20001–2085

The Children's Aid Society
105 E. 22nd Street
New York, NY 10010

Epilepsy Foundation of America
1828 L Street, Suite 406
Washington, D.C. 20036

Girl Scouts of the U.S.A.
420 Fifth Avenue
New York, NY 10018

Handicapped Equestrian Learning Program (HELP)
2908-B Gregg Lane
Manor, TX 78653

Organizations That Help Children
(continued)

The Hole-in-the-Wall Gang Camp Fund
555 Long Wharf Drive
New Haven, CT 06511

Juvenile Diabetes Foundation
23 E. 26th Street
New York, NY 10010

Leukemia Society of America
800 Second Avenue
New York, NY 10017

Make a Wish Foundation
2600 N. Central Avenue, Suite 936
Phoenix, AZ 85016

March of Dimes
1275 Mamaroneck Avenue
White Plains, NY 10605

National Association of the Deaf
814 Thayer Avenue
Silver Spring, MD 20910

The National Easter Seal Society
230 W. Monroe, 18th Floor
Chicago, IL 60603

National Reye's Syndrome Foundation
426 N. Lewis St.
Bryan, OH 43506

Save the Children
P.O. Box 925
Westport, CT 06881

Special Olympics, Inc.
1701 K Street, N.W., Suite 203
Washington, D.C. 20006

United Cerebral Palsy Association, Inc.
66 E. 34th Street
New York, NY 10016

U.S. Committee for UNICEF
333 E. 38th Street
New York, NY 10016

Where to Start

If you decide to help an older person, here are some of the people, places, and organizations that can put you in touch with someone who needs your help.

PEOPLE

- doctors
- neighbors
- social workers
- priests, ministers, rabbis, or other clergy

PLACES

- convalescent homes
- hospitals
- nursing homes
- recreation departments
- rehabilitation centers
- retirement communities
- senior centers

ORGANIZATIONS

- area agencies on aging
- home health agencies
- senior citizen service organizations listed in the Yellow Pages of your telephone directory

> One thing I know: the only ones among you who will be really happy are those who have sought and found how to serve.
> —*Albert Schweitzer*

Things to Think About

Here are some things to keep in mind when helping senior citizens:

- Always call to set up an appointment time before going to visit. Don't promise to visit and then fail to show up. This can be tremendously disappointing. If for some reason you are unable to come, get in touch with your friend as soon as possible and apologize.

- If you plan to take food, make sure you know about any dietary restrictions or special needs.

- Some older people tire easily and need to take naps during the day. If your friend gets sleepy during your visit, ask if he or she would like you to leave and return at another time.

- Everyone loves surprises: Each time you visit, bring something to show to your friend—a baby picture of yourself, a project you are working on, a new electronic gadget, or rocks or shells that you have collected. These can be great conversation starters.

Things to Think About
(continued)

- If the person you are helping has lost one of his or her senses, such as sight, smell, or hearing, think of creative ways to reach his or her other senses. For example, if you are helping a person who has lost the sense of sight, you might want to bring fragrant flowers for the person to smell or something with a lot of texture to touch. For a person who is deaf or hard of hearing, remember to talk louder than you usually do and sit or stand where he or she can read your lips.

- Many seniors enjoy books with large print. They also may enjoy listening to music and books on tape. You can find these books and tapes at most public libraries.

- Visit as often as you can. These times together can be special for both of you.

Serve as a Secretary

Be a secretary for someone who has difficulty writing. Ask if the person would like to dictate a letter to a family member or friend while you write for him or her. When you are finished, read the letter aloud to make sure that it is accurate.

Address an envelope, donate a stamp, and mail the letter.

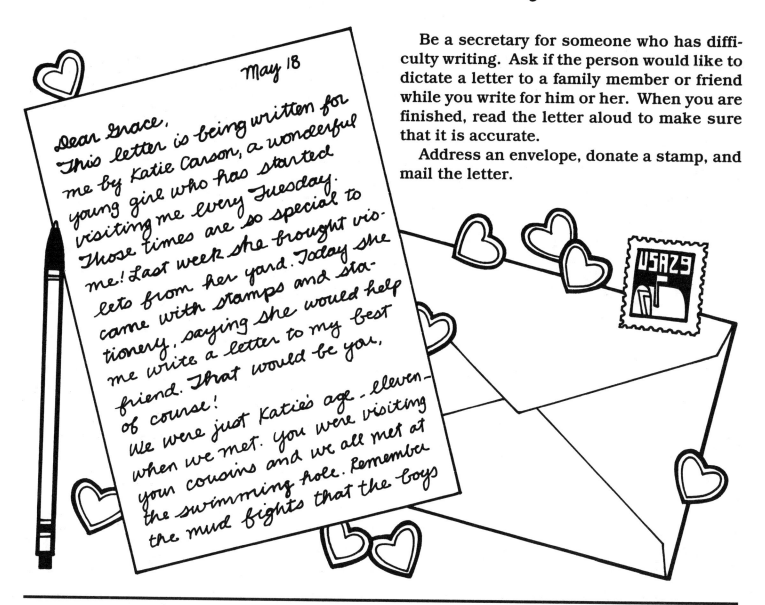

May 18

Dear Grace,

This letter is being written for me by Katie Carson, a wonderful young girl who has started visiting me every Tuesday. Those times are so special to me! Last week she brought violets from her yard. Today she came with stamps and stationery, saying she would help me write a letter to my best friend. That would be you, of course!

We were just Katie's age - eleven - when we met. You were visiting your cousins and we all met at the swimming hole. Remember the mud fights that the boys

Play a Game

Challenge the person you visit in a hospital, nursing home, or retirement home to a game of checkers, chess, or cards. Another idea is to bring along your favorite board game to play. You might even ask the person you are visiting to teach *you* a game.

Adopt a Grandparent

Many elderly people are separated from family members who live far away. They may have few visitors and little chance to interact with young people and teenagers. Here is an ideal way for younger and older people to share time together.

Find a senior citizen in your community who would like a regular visitor. Make a commitment to yourself to visit this person at regularly scheduled times. Between visits, keep in touch with notes and phone calls.

The idea behind this project is to offer your company to a person who might be lonely and would enjoy visits from you. Friendship with an older person can enrich your life because most older people have experiences, memories, and wisdom to share with you. At holiday times, you'll have someone special to remember, and you'll learn from each other during your visits throughout the year.

Read Aloud

Many elderly people have difficulty reading the small print in books and newspapers. While there are books with large type available in libraries, not everyone has easy access to them. Spend time reading aloud to a person from a book by a favorite author, a collection of poetry, a local newspaper, or a magazine.

This is a great way for you to practice your oral reading skills. At the same time, you'll have a chance to bring pleasure to someone who loves books and misses being able to read.

> Just the knowledge that a good book is awaiting one at the end of a long day makes that day happier.
> —Kathleen Norris

Brown Bag a Lunch

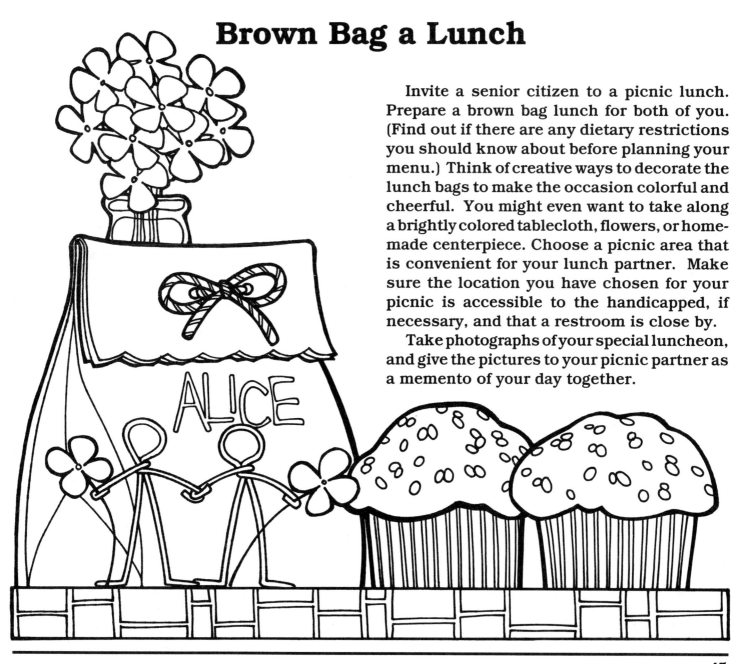

Invite a senior citizen to a picnic lunch. Prepare a brown bag lunch for both of you. (Find out if there are any dietary restrictions you should know about before planning your menu.) Think of creative ways to decorate the lunch bags to make the occasion colorful and cheerful. You might even want to take along a brightly colored tablecloth, flowers, or home-made centerpiece. Choose a picnic area that is convenient for your lunch partner. Make sure the location you have chosen for your picnic is accessible to the handicapped, if necessary, and that a restroom is close by.

Take photographs of your special luncheon, and give the pictures to your picnic partner as a memento of your day together.

Plan an Interview

Some elderly people like to tell about special events in their lives. Most of them would welcome spending time talking to a young person about their accomplishments in life. Arrange an interview with an older person. Make a list of questions you want to ask so you are well prepared. (See the suggestions on page 47.) Write the answers down, or bring along a tape recorder to use if the person has no objections.

When the interview is over, plan a creative way to use the information you have gathered.

- For example, if the person you talked with gives you permission, share your findings with your friends so they can learn about the person you interviewed. You can also invite them to meet your senior friend.

- Another idea is to make a birthday card filled with fun facts about the person you interviewed. You can also write a poem for the person you interviewed using information you gathered.

Ideas for Interview Questions

EARLY YEARS

1. Where did you grow up?

2. Did you have a pet as a child? If so, what kind?

3. What special memories do you have of your childhood and family members?

4. What things did you and your family enjoy doing together?

5. How were birthdays and holidays celebrated in your home? Which holiday was your favorite?

EDUCATION, CAREER, AND FAMILY

1. Where did you go to school?

2. What were your favorite subjects in school?

3. Who influenced your life the most?

4. What made you choose the job you have or had?

5. What did you like most about your work? What did you like least?

6. Do you have children? Grandchildren? What are their names and ages?

7. What unusual places have you and your family visited?

SPECIAL INTERESTS

1. What hobbies and special interests do you enjoy in your spare time?

2. What three words best describe you?

3. What advice would you give young people today?

Create a Story

A variation of the interview described on page 46 is to create a story for a senior citizen based on an actual incident in his or her life. First, set a time to interview your friend. During the interview, focus on one topic to write about. Here are some suggestions for topics:

- a happy childhood memory

- a funny incident

- a great achievement

Use your interview notes to write a short biography based on the facts you learned about this person's life.

Next, using unlined white art paper, illustrate two or three parts of the story. You can either draw these pictures using colored pencils, markers, or crayons, or you can cut pictures from old magazines. Make a front and back cover for your illustrated story from colored construction paper.

Think of a title for your story, and list your name as author and illustrator. Write a dedication to your friend on the inside front cover, and present the story to him or her as a special gift.

TANGERINE

TWO GEESE,
A
WATERMELON,
AND A
WAGON WHEEL

A STORY FROM THE
LIFE OF ED BABCOCK

CHOCOLATE

RUST

PEACH

TURQUOISE

Share a Talent

Think about a special talent you have—something that you do well and enjoy sharing with others. It might be playing a musical instrument, singing, dancing, or acting. Plan to perform for people in a nursing or convalescent home.

You can also organize a talent show. Ask classmates and friends to come along and add their talents. Try to get a wide variety of acts. Consider asking a music or drama teacher to help you arrange a special performance. Plan several rehearsals so your talent show runs smoothly. You might want to distribute a simple program listing the various acts and the names of all the performers.

After your show, talk to the people you performed for and try to discover special interests and talents *they* might have. Perhaps you can make arrangements for one of them to visit your class, scout troop, or youth service group to share a special interest or talent in return.

Lend a Hand

Volunteer your services and help a senior citizen who lives alone. Here are some ways you might help:

- change lightbulbs
- wash a car
- dust and vacuum
- mow a lawn or rake leaves
- hang pictures
- wash windows and screens
- plant flowers or weed a garden
- arrange photo albums
- cook a favorite meal or dish
- rearrange a closet
- care for houseplants
- polish silver

If an adult can provide transportation:

- accompany a senior citizen to a doctor's appointment
- take broken appliances to be fixed
- run errands such as buying stamps, picking up a prescription, or shopping for groceries
- take a senior citizen to visit a friend he or she hasn't seen in a long time

The things to do are the things that need doing that you see need to be done and that no one else seems to see need to be done.
—*R. Buckminster Fuller*

Be a Pen Pal

Be a pen pal to a senior citizen. Receiving cards, letters, and notes brightens a person's day and lets the person know he or she is cared about. You may also want to enclose poetry and short stories you clip from magazines or creative writing and art projects you have done at school.

Fill a Basket

Show you care by making a gift basket for a senior citizen. You can pick a holiday theme for your basket, such as Valentine's Day, Thanksgiving, Christmas, or Hanukkah. You can give a basket as a birthday or an anniversary present. You can also make a basket that recognizes a special interest of an older person such as . . .

a book lover's basket filled with

- new or used hardcover or paperback books
- magazines (collected from your family and friends)
- a bookmark made by you

a letter writer's basket filled with

- note cards
- stationery
- postage stamps
- envelopes
- a pen

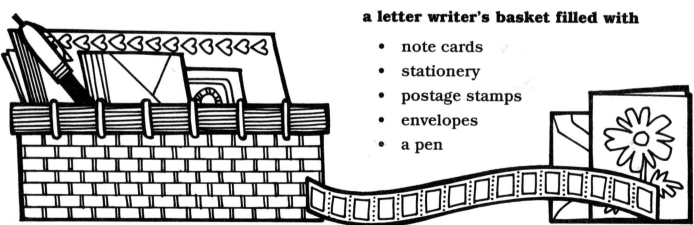

Fill a Basket
(continued)

a bath basket filled with

- scented soaps
- a bath sponge
- bubble bath
- a wash cloth
- dusting powder

a kitchen basket filled with

- potholders
- wooden spoons
- recipe cards
- an ingredient for one of the recipes

a gardener's basket filled with

- gardening gloves
- flower pots
- seeds to plant
- small gardening tools

Send a Balloon-o-Gram

Visit a senior who is living alone in your neighborhood or one who is in a hospital, a retirement home, or a convalescent facility. Bring along a balloon with a special coupon inside. The coupon can be redeemed at a later date for a service provided by you.

Copy the coupon below and fill it out using one of the ideas listed or one you create yourself. Fold the coupon, and place it in the balloon before you fill the balloon with air or helium. Add colorful ribbon streamers to the end of your balloon.

Get your friends, family, or classmates to join you in the project, and present a whole bouquet of balloons filled with coupons to make lots of seniors happy!

Ideas for coupons:

- good for a video rental

- good for a batch of my homemade chocolate chip cookies

- good for two weeks of plant care

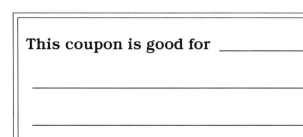

This coupon is good for _____

_____

_____

Kids Who Care

Jonathan Akchin is 12 years old and is in the seventh grade in Stevenson, Maryland.

Jonathan's school requires all students to complete 40 hours of community service in order to graduate. So Jonathan called the director of the nursing home across the street from his home and asked if he could help. Jonathan made an appointment to meet the activities director who introduced him to some of the residents and told him how he could help. Now Jonathan visits the nursing home every Sunday and on weekdays when school is out. He takes coffee and hot chocolate to the residents' rooms, calls off the numbers in bingo, delivers mail, and visits with the residents. Sometimes he even brings his cockatiel, Casey, with him.

Jonathan met his 40-hour community service requirement a long time ago, but he still visits the nursing home at least once a week and has no plans to stop.

Stephen Wright is 10 years old and is in the fourth grade in Irvine, California.

Stephen and his mom belong to an organization that helps elderly people. They visit the same nursing home regularly and get to know the people who live there. Stephen especially likes sharing holidays with his friends at the nursing home. They have parties for holidays such as Halloween and Cinco de Mayo. Stephen and his mom bring special food, gifts, games, and music to the people who live in the nursing home. He says the residents really enjoy the visits and the parties, and he learns a lot from having older friends.

Organizations That Help the Elderly

AARP (American Association of Retired Persons)
601 E Street N.W.
Washington, D.C. 20049

Alzheimer's Disease & Related Disorders Association, Inc.
919 N. Michigan Avenue
Chicago, IL 60611

American Aging Association
2129 Providence Avenue
Chester, PA 19013

American Geriatrics Society
770 Lexington Avenue, Suite 300
New York, NY 10021

Arthritis Foundation
1314 Spring Street N.W.
Atlanta, GA 30309

Disabled American Veterans
807 Maine Avenue S.W.
Washington, D.C. 20024

Gray Panthers Project Fund
2025 Pennsylvania Avenue N.W.
Suite 821
Washington, D.C. 20006

Check the Yellow Pages under Senior Citizens' Services & Organizations for local organizations and senior centers.

Things to Think About

Anyone can find themselves in need at one time or another. Natural disasters such as floods, hurricanes, earthquakes, or fires may unexpectedly leave an individual or family homeless and stranded without any personal possessions.

Other people may find themselves in need for different reasons. There are probably people in your community who have had very hard lives and could use a helping hand. Some of these people may have lost their jobs and are having difficulty finding work. Some may find themselves homeless. Others may be ill or may have a family member who is suffering from a chronic illness.

These situations provide numerous opportunities for you to help others. Think of ways you can help a neighbor or community member who has been struck by a disaster. It might be baby-sitting the kids while the parents take care of business, or making sandwiches to take to families cleaning up after a catastrophe.

In this section, you'll find many suggestions for ways to help people in need and brighten their days.

Some people see things as they are and say "Why?" I dream things that never were and say "Why not?"
—*George Bernard Shaw*

Round Up Sports Equipment

Save your old skateboard, baseball bat, catcher's mitt, volleyball, football, and other sports equipment instead of throwing it away once you've outgrown it. There are lots of people in your community who would love to have the equipment you no longer play with.

Organize a sports equipment roundup week. Ask friends, classmates, and neighbors to add to your equipment collection. The items you collect will provide hours of fun and recreation for kids in a preschool or for people in a homeless shelter.

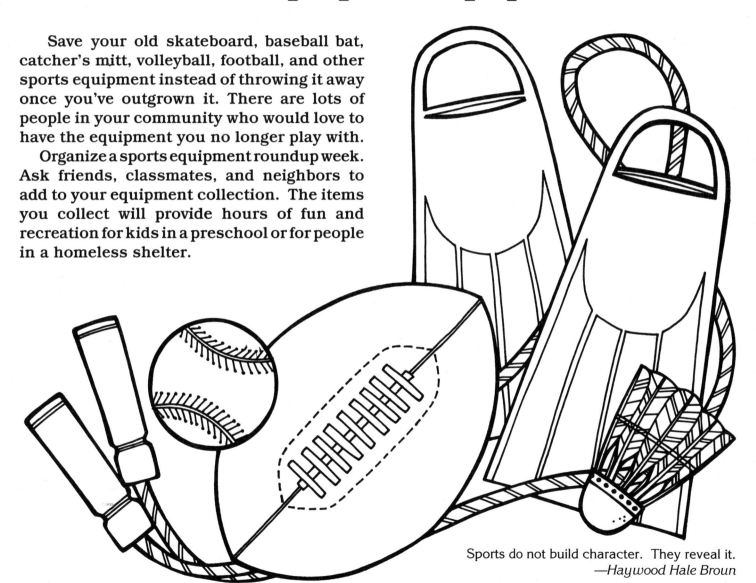

Sports do not build character. They reveal it.
—*Haywood Hale Broun*

Scavenger Hunt for Food

Looking for a different "twist" for your next party? Here's an idea that's not only fun but is a great opportunity to help people in need in your community.

Divide your guests into teams of four or five players. Give each team a list of items to find as they go from house to house in your neighborhood. You can use the list on the following page or create your own.

Ask each team to go to a different area to avoid several teams asking for food at the same house. Team members should be told not to go into anyone's house. Be sure an adult is along to supervise each group.

As you go to each house, ask for a few of the items on your list. Be sure to explain that you are collecting the food to help people in need. Thank the person for any food that is donated.

Determine a time limit for the scavenger hunt (about 30 minutes) and plan to meet back at the party. Give a prize to the team that brings back the most items on the scavenger hunt list.

Ask your mom or dad to drive you to an agency or organization that distributes food to individuals and families needing assistance. Enclose a note explaining the scavenger hunt, and include it with the food you collected at your party.

Ideas for Scavenger Hunt

Soups

- ❑ broccoli
- ❑ chicken broth
- ❑ chicken noodle
- ❑ chicken rice
- ❑ mushroom
- ❑ tomato
- ❑ vegetable

Canned Vegetables

- ❑ asparagus
- ❑ baked beans
- ❑ beets
- ❑ carrots
- ❑ corn
- ❑ green beans
- ❑ lima beans
- ❑ peas
- ❑ pumpkin

Canned Fruit

- ❑ applesauce
- ❑ apricots
- ❑ fruit cocktail
- ❑ peaches
- ❑ pears
- ❑ pineapple

Miscellaneous

- ❑ baby food
- ❑ bread
- ❑ cereal
- ❑ cocoa mix
- ❑ coffee
- ❑ condiments
- ❑ cookies
- ❑ crackers
- ❑ dried fruit
- ❑ fruit juice
- ❑ jelly and jam
- ❑ oatmeal
- ❑ pasta
- ❑ peanut butter
- ❑ powdered milk
- ❑ rice
- ❑ salad dressing
- ❑ spaghetti sauce
- ❑ tea
- ❑ tomato sauce
- ❑ vegetable juice

Main Dishes

- ❑ chili
- ❑ ravioli
- ❑ stew
- ❑ tuna

Share a Celebration

Start a new tradition in your family. The next time anyone has a birthday and celebrates by having a party, ask each guest to bring a wrapped gift for a person in need. It could be a gift of nonperishable food, a household item, clothing, books, toys, or bath items.

Let the "party person" have the fun of unwrapping each donated gift.

After the party, donate the gifts to an agency that helps people in need. Think how many people could be helped if some of your party guests started the same tradition in their own families!

Clean Your Closet

Recycle clothes you've outgrown by donating them to a shelter or to a program in your community that helps homeless children. Get other family members to clean their closets, too. You might also ask your teacher if you can organize a "Clean Your Closet Week" for your class. All of the clothes you and your classmates collect can be donated to people in need.

To add a personal touch, pick one article of clothing from those you are donating. Write a short note telling about something special that happened while you were wearing this article of clothing. Attach your note to the piece of clothing, or tuck it in a pocket for the new owner to find.

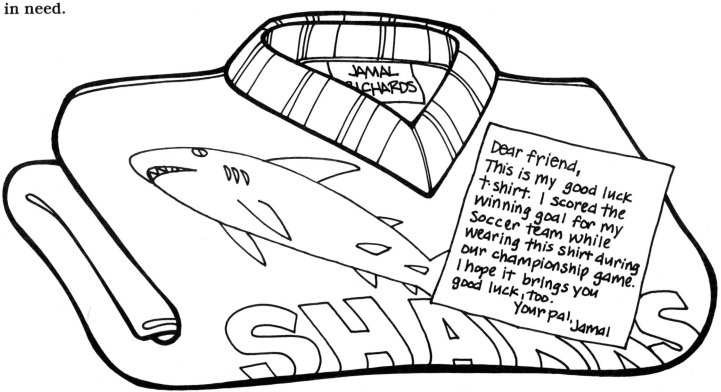

Grow a Garden

Ask your teacher if your class can plant a fruit and vegetable garden and donate the food it produces to a worthy cause. Once you get an okay, here's what you do.

Find a suitable area at school for your garden. Decide what kinds of fruits and vegetables you could plant such as cucumbers, tomatoes, carrots, radishes, strawberries, or melons. Ask someone from a nursery to give you tips on how to properly plant and care for your garden. Divide the tasks of planting and tending the garden among your classmates.

When your fruits and vegetables are ready to be enjoyed, donate the food to a shelter in your community. You can also make a salad for the residents of a shelter to enjoy.

Give a Gift Certificate

Has a person ever approached you or someone in your family and asked for money to buy food? If you're with your mom or dad and you agree that you would like to help, here's an idea. Instead of giving money and not being sure of how the money will be spent, give a gift certificate to a fast-food restaurant or coffee shop. The person will get a hot meal, and you'll have the satisfaction of helping a person in need.

Look on pages 119–144 for some fun ways to raise money. Use the money you collect to purchase the gift certificates.

Assist After a Disaster

Lend a helping hand following a natural disaster such as an earthquake, a hurricane, a flood, a wildfire, a mudslide, or a tornado. There are many ways you can help and make a difference to people who have lost many of their possessions and/or have had damage to their homes.

raise money to help a family in your community

donate clothes and toys

collect and distribute blankets

make sandwiches and serve them to rescue workers and volunteers

make and put up posters for lost pets

help with clean-up operations once the area has been declared safe

Kids Who Care

Billy Peevey is 10 years old and is in the fifth grade in Garland, Texas.

With his Boy Scout troop, Billy has helped people in many ways. His favorite activity was Scouting for Food, a project of Boy Scout troops throughout north Texas. The boys collected food for homeless shelters and food banks at the time of year when it was needed most—in February. Food banks and shelters get lots of food donations around the holidays, but when that food runs out, many run short for the rest of the year. Scouting for Food was so successful that the donated food lasted until the next holiday season!

Here's how Scouting for Food worked: A local TV station told viewers that they would find empty bags on their front doors. They were asked to put nonperishable food in the bags to be donated to people in need. Each Boy Scout was assigned to place bags on the front doors of every home on certain streets and to go back at a certain time to pick up the food. The food was taken to a nearby food bank or shelter.

Sacha Bice is 15 years old and is in the 8th grade in Fullerton, California.

Sacha is raising a puppy to be a guide dog for a person who is visually impaired. She started raising puppies as a 4-H project. She liked the idea of raising an animal that would help someone have a better life.

The first puppy Sacha raised was a golden retriever named Neon. He didn't have the right temperament to become a guide dog, but Sacha was able to find a good home for him. Now she's raising her second pup, Lando. Sacha trains him to sit, stay, heel, and obey other commands. When she goes out, she frequently brings Lando with her so that he gets used to being around many different people.

When he's ready, Lando will go to "college" for advanced training. Although Sacha says it will be difficult to say goodbye to him, she knows that he will be providing important assistance and friendship for someone who needs him.

Organizations That Help People in Need

American Red Cross
17th and D Streets N.W.
Washington, D.C. 20006

B'nai B'rith International
1640 Rhode Island Avenue N.W.
Washington, D.C. 20036-3278

CARE
151 Ellis Street
Atlanta, GA 30303

Catholic Charities USA
1731 King Street
Alexandria, VA 22314

Family Service America
11700 W. Lake Park Drive
Park Place
Milwaukee, WI 53224

National Legal Aid and Defender Association
1625 K Street N.W., Suite 800
Washington, D.C. 20006

The National Literacy Hotline Contact Center, Inc.
P.O. Box 81826
Lincoln, NE 68501

Oxfam America
115 Broadway
Boston, MA 02116

The Salvation Army
615 Slaters Lane
Alexandria, VA 22313

United Way of America
701 N. Fairfax Street
Alexandria, VA 22314

Volunteers of America
3813 N. Causeway Boulevard
Metairie, LA 70002

Helping Animals

Where to Start

If you decide to become involved in helping animals, here are some of the people, places, and organizations you may wish to contact.

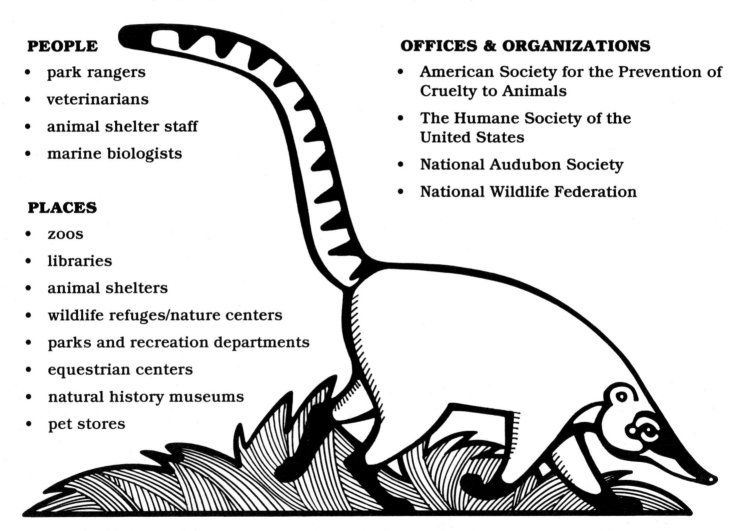

PEOPLE

- park rangers
- veterinarians
- animal shelter staff
- marine biologists

PLACES

- zoos
- libraries
- animal shelters
- wildlife refuges/nature centers
- parks and recreation departments
- equestrian centers
- natural history museums
- pet stores

OFFICES & ORGANIZATIONS

- American Society for the Prevention of Cruelty to Animals
- The Humane Society of the United States
- National Audubon Society
- National Wildlife Federation

Know What's Happening

Animals affect our lives in many ways—and we affect theirs. Almost every day, newspapers contain articles about animals: birds caught in an oil spill, a law to protect wild horses, a "pet" wolf that has turned dangerous, raccoons causing problems in the suburbs, coral reef destruction, and a litter of kittens abandoned in a dumpster. Newspapers may also contain letters to the editor on local or global situations.

By reading the newspaper, you can be informed about animal problems and can spread the word to others. Why not start an "Animals in the News" scrapbook or classroom bulletin board? If you want to get involved in the situations you have learned about, contact your local humane society or nature center, or one of the organizations listed at the end of this chapter.

Make a Present for a Pet

Create some of these simple toys for animals at a Humane Society shelter, a classroom pet, pets belonging to your friends and neighbors, or your own critters.

Tie a tennis ball inside an old sock for tossing and tugging games.

Make a kitty "fishing pole" from a stick, a string, and a piece of paper. (Waxed paper and cellophane are good noisemakers!)

Plant grass or birdseed in a margarine tub, and let your parakeet or cat nibble the greens.

Make a rattle for a rabbit by taping a few buttons or pebbles inside a small juice can.

Make a hamster ladder by gluing ice cream sticks to a piece of cardboard.

Cardboard tubes and oatmeal boxes make great tunnels for little critters.

Make a Present for a Pet
(continued)

Create a cat clubhouse from an old carton. Cut windows and doors and add decorations.

More cat toys: a ball of tinfoil to swat and a small stuffed sock to chase and "attack."

Cats, rabbits, and guinea pigs love to play in paper bags.

Make a dog tug-o-war toy from old nylons knotted together.

Make a fun tunnel for guinea pigs from a large can that is open at both ends and an old sweatshirt sleeve or a big old sock with the toe cut off. Tape the sleeve or sock to the can.

Rats like to play in baskets or cardboard tubes hung from the top of the cage.

Help at an Animal Shelter

Many communities have facilities that provide care for animals that are lost, abused, or unwanted. Visit one or more of these shelters, and learn about the work that is done there. Services offered by animal shelters vary widely. Some shelters deal only with pets; others handle livestock and/or wildlife. They may offer an education program or veterinary clinic.

If you want to help, ask the shelter staff about the opportunities available for volunteers. Some possibilities are listed below.

- feeding, grooming, and exercising animals

- cleaning cages; keeping the grounds and buildings neat and clean

- making posters or putting up bulletin boards to teach shelter visitors about animals and animal-related problems

- helping with fund-raising projects or special events

DOG WALK·A·THON
SATURDAY, JUNE 12
PROCEEDS BENEFIT SANTA MARIA S.P.C.A.

Be a Zoo Helper

Many zoos have student volunteer programs. If there is a zoo in your community, find out how you can participate in such a program. If there isn't one, find out if a nature center, an aquarium, or a wildlife refuge could use your help.

Provide Water for Wildlife

In hot, dry weather, setting out water for animals will make them more comfortable and may save their lives. This can be done in your yard or a vacant lot, or with permission in a park or at your school.

A shallow dish of water set among plants or rocks will give lizards a place to get a drink or toads a place to soak.

Lost dogs, stray cats, and animals such as raccoons and opossums can drink from deeper dishes.

Place a long stick in each dish of water so that if a small animal falls in, it will be able to escape.

Provide Water for Wildlife
(continued)

Make a shower for birds by poking a tiny nail hole in a plastic jug, filling the jug with water and hanging it above a birdbath. Birds love to play in the drips!

Do not place birdbaths next to bushes where cats can hide.

Check containers frequently to make sure that that they contain clean, fresh water. The animals will be glad you did!

Go to Bat for Bats

These fascinating, misunderstood animals—found in all but the very hottest and coldest parts of the world—are crucial to the ecosystem. Many wild tropical plants depend on bats for pollination. In rain forests, flying bats disperse seeds to areas where the land has been cleared so new growth can begin. The bats from one cave in Texas eat approximately 150 tons of insects nightly!

Unfortunately, bats face many dangers, including pesticide poisoning, habitat destruction, and the disturbance of their in-cave colonies by malicious or careless people. (A human walking into the cave can cause fatal stress in hibernating bats or can make nonhibernating bats abandon their babies.) Several species of bats found in the United States have become endangered.

For information on how you can help these helpful creatures, write to

Bat Conservation International
P.O. Box 162603
Austin, TX 78716

Fight Pet Overpopulation

Although animal shelters in this country are overflowing with unwanted pets, many people allow their dogs and cats to continue breeding. This results in millions of healthy, friendly animals which must be destroyed because there are no homes for them. *Every minute*, 40 dogs, cats, puppies, and kittens must be put to death. There are simply no homes for them, no places for them to go.

What can be done about this terrible problem? Dog and cat owners must be told about it and encouraged to have their pets spayed (if they are female) or neutered (if they are male). Spaying and neutering are simple operations done by a veterinarian that prevent animals from producing offspring.

You can educate people by making a poster like the one shown here. Illustrate your poster with photos of 40 dogs, cats, puppies, and kittens cut from magazines. If you prefer, you can draw your own pictures.

Perhaps your local humane society would like to display this poster at their shelter or use it as part of an education program. It could also be effective if posted in a pet shop or veterinarian's office. Get permission before hanging up your poster.

Care for a Classroom Pet

Many teachers enjoy having pets in their classrooms but are too busy to give the regular care and attention that animals need. Perhaps you could help care for a classroom pet in your school, at a preschool, or at a day-care center. Your responsibilities might include providing food and water, cleaning the cage or bedding, exercising or playing with the animal, and/or taking it home on weekends. Before offering to care for a pet, get permission from your parents. Take time to learn what the pet's needs are. Most libraries have good books on pet care.

If a teacher agrees to let you help care for a pet, write down the things you will be expected to do. Find out if the animal has any habits or special requirements you should know about (fears, food allergies, favorite toys). Caring for pets can be fun, but it's also a big responsibility. Think carefully about this before promising to help.

Kids Who Care

Some kids who care in New York came up with a fun way to raise money to help endangered animals. You can do the same thing. Begin by doing some research on endangered animals. Select one and make a papier-mâché model of the animal. It could be a snow leopard, a gray wolf, a gorilla, or any other endangered animal. Take the model into your school cafeteria at lunch time. Have kids pay for a chance to play a guessing game. For example, have them guess how many peanuts or pieces of wrapped candy are in a jar. Give a stuffed animal to the person whose guess is the closest, and give the money you collect to an organization that helps endangered animals.

Katy McKean is 9 years old and is in the third grade in Austin, Texas.

Katy likes helping animals, partly because animals help Katy, too! Katy has oralmotor apraxia, which means that some of her muscles don't work well. She rides horses at the Handicapped Equestrian Learning Program as a fun form of physical therapy. She assists in taking care of the horses by grooming them, helping to shoe them, giving them water, and putting blankets on them.

Katy and her family also take in and care for abandoned animals until new homes can be found for them.

Organizations That Help Animals

American Humane Association
P.O. Box 1266
Denver, CO 80201–1266

American Society for the Prevention of Cruelty to Animals
424 E. 92nd Street
New York, NY 10128
Attention: Education Department

Animal Welfare Institute
P.O. Box 3650
Washington, D.C. 20007

Defenders of Wildlife
1244 19th Street N.W.
Washington, D.C. 20036

Focus on Animals
P.O. Box 150
Trumball, CT 06611

Friends of Animals
P.O. Box 1244
Norwalk, CT 06856

Humane Society of the United States
2100 L Street N.W.
Washington, D.C. 20037

International Fund for Animal Welfare
Box 193
Yarmouth Port, MA 02675

National Humane Education Society
15-B Catoctin Circle S.E., #207
Leesburg, VA 22075

Performing Animal Welfare Society
P.O. Box 842
Galt, CA 95632

Save the Dolphins Project
Earth Island Institute
300 Broadway, Suite 28
San Francisco, CA 94133

Society for Animal Protective Legislation
P.O. Box 3719
Washington, D.C. 20007

Student Action Corps for Animals
P.O. Box 15588
Washington, D.C. 20003

FIRE DEPARTMENT

 4H MEETS HERE

 YMCA

 BOTANIC GARDEN

Helping Your Community

ART CENTER

 CITY HALL

 SIERRA MIDDLE SCHOOL

 RED CROSS

GOLDEN OAKS SENIOR CENTER

 NATURAL HISTORY MUSEUM

Lawndale Library

 Recreation Department
CITY OF CHESTERTON

 HOSPITAL

Where to Start

Here are some of the people, places, and organizations that might need your help or could put you in touch with someone who could use assistance in your community.

PEOPLE

- principals/teachers
- ministers/rabbis/priests
- neighbors/friends
- doctors/nurses
- social workers
- librarians
- police officers
- fire fighters

PLACES

- schools
- hospitals
- libraries
- museums
- police and fire departments
- parks and recreation departments
- places of worship
- senior centers

OFFICES AND ORGANIZATIONS

- government agencies
- American Red Cross
- Girls Incorporated
- Camp Fire Boys and Girls
- 4-H
- Big Brothers/Sisters
- family service agencies
- community service organizations
- Boy Scouts/Girl Scouts

MARINE MUSEUM →
COMMUNITY CENTER ↑
BIRD SANCTUARY ↗

Beautify Your School

Your school is an important part of your community, whether you attend a rural one-room schoolhouse, a large inner-city school, or a school nestled in a suburban neighborhood. Since you spend so much of your time at school, why not form a committee to help beautify your campus?

Start by getting permission from your teacher or principal. Perhaps your whole class can get involved with the project. You can also ask for student volunteers from each grade level at your school. Considering asking teachers or parents to join your group.

Once your committee is formed, take a tour around your school to find areas that need beautifying. You might discover an area that is overgrown with weeds and needs clearing, or a spot that could use some plants to perk it up.

A group of students and parents from Dos Pueblos High School in Goleta, California did just that! They identified a drop-off area in the front of the school that was just dirt and weeds. They formed a "Beautify Dos Pueblos" committee and selected that area as their first project.

A few months later, after soliciting donations and help from other students and families and from the owners of local nurseries, the driveway is now lined with trees and is blooming with yellow and blue flowers, the school's team colors. The improvement goes a long way in the feeling of pride the students have for their school.

What could you do to help beautify your school campus?

Stuff Envelopes

Nonprofit organizations that serve your community usually do several mailings throughout the year. Some of these mailings are to solicit funds for their causes. Other mailings are pamphlets sent to people who request information about the goals and objectives of the organization. Information about special activities and projects that the organization is sponsoring also requires mailings.

Since most fliers must be folded and placed in envelopes, the preparation of these mailings is time-consuming. Choose an organization you would like to help, and call their office to let them know you are available to stuff envelopes for them. Ask some of your friends to volunteer their time, too. Stuffing envelopes with a group can be fun!

Buy a Book

Most libraries cannot afford to buy all the books they would like to make available to their patrons. Here's a great project that you and your friends can do to get more books for your local library.

To start, ask librarians to make a "wish list" of children's books they would like to order but don't have sufficient funds to purchase. Then, with the librarians' permission, schedule a "Buy a Book Week." Talk to the owner or manager of a bookstore in your community. Ask him or her to lend you the books on the "wish list." Set up a display at the library including the books and a poster announcing "Buy a Book Week." Use removable labels to mark the price on each book.

The poster should explain that library patrons are a being asked to donate money to purchase the books that are displayed. Tell patrons how and where to make their donation. For example, you could ask the reference librarian, children's librarian, or another library staff member to be in charge of collecting donations. Also mention that in return for the donation, a special label will be placed inside the front cover of the book. The label will display the name of the person who donated the money to purchase the book.

When someone donates money for a book, mark that book "purchased." At the end of the week, return any unsold books to the bookstore, along with the money that was donated to buy the books.

Write a Letter to a Leader

Often you will see or hear about things in your community that need attention. You can help by writing to your congressional representative, mayor, city council representatives, or other elected officials concerning these issues. Ask questions about what is currently being done, and make constructive suggestions for addressing these issues. Volunteer to help and become involved.

Once you get a response to your letter, share it with your parents, your teacher, or your classmates. Do you think the response addressed your concerns? What is the next step you could take to deal with this issue?

Helpful Hints

- To get the names and addresses of your mayor, city council members, and other local government officials, call your local city hall. It is usually listed in the "Government Listings" section in the front of your telephone book under "Local Government Offices" or "City Government Offices."

- To get the names and addresses of state and federal government officials (including your U.S. Senators and U.S. Representatives to Congress), call the local office of the League of Women Voters. It is usually listed in the White Pages of your telephone book.

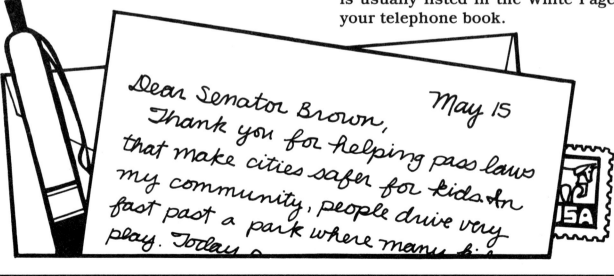

Plan an Appreciation Day

Set aside a special day each month to show your appreciation for a person who has made your community a better place in which to live.

You might choose to honor a school crossing guard, a fire fighter, your principal, a police officer, a teacher or coach, or a favorite librarian.

On appreciation day, do special things for the person you selected. Bake a batch of cookies or make a personalized gift. Include a thank-you card to let the person know how much you appreciate all he or she has done for your community. You could even write a letter about the person's contributions to your community and submit it to the editor of your local newspaper.

Help Serve Food

Volunteer with your friends or family members to help at a community shelter. You can help serve meals and clean up when the meal is over.

After the meal, take time to talk and play with younger children at the facility. You might want to bring along a favorite book or game to share. When you return to school, tell your classmates about your experience. Find out if they are interested in organizing a class project to help at a shelter throughout the school year.

Organize a Sing-Along

Organize a sing-along at a convalescent hospital, a nursery school, a community center, a shopping mall, a homeless shelter, or a senior citizen center. Make a sing-along program with the words to popular tunes, and distribute copies to the participants. While you may want to organize your sing-along around a holiday theme, this event can be planned for any time during the year.

Make a First Aid Kit

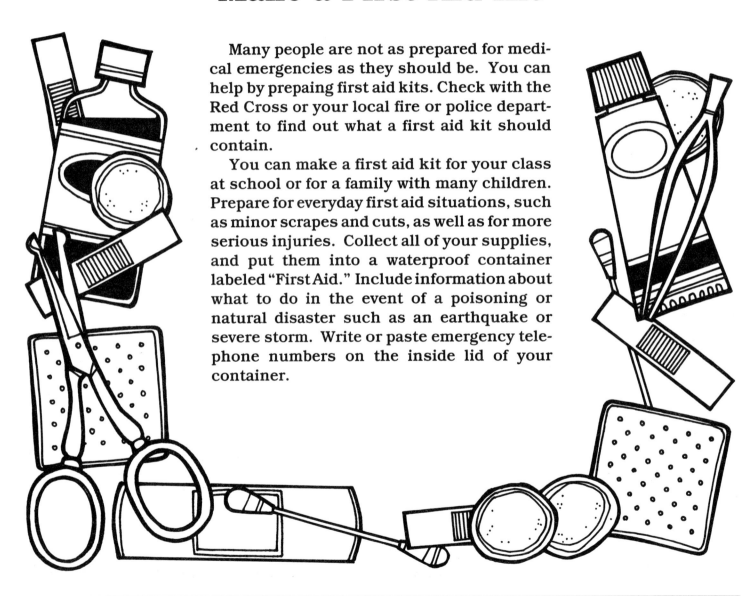

Many people are not as prepared for medical emergencies as they should be. You can help by prepaing first aid kits. Check with the Red Cross or your local fire or police department to find out what a first aid kit should contain.

You can make a first aid kit for your class at school or for a family with many children. Prepare for everyday first aid situations, such as minor scrapes and cuts, as well as for more serious injuries. Collect all of your supplies, and put them into a waterproof container labeled "First Aid." Include information about what to do in the event of a poisoning or natural disaster such as an earthquake or severe storm. Write or paste emergency telephone numbers on the inside lid of your container.

Provide Emergency Information

It is important that children know what they can and should do in an emergency situation. You can help your community by making a mini-poster or flyer to show younger children what to do in an emergency.

To get the most current information, write or talk to someone at your local police or fire department. Make a rough draft of your poster, and ask this person to check your information for accuracy. Keep the information simple and easy for young kids to understand. Be sure to include instructions for dialing 9-1-1. Think of a good way for young children to memorize their address and phone number. You could, for example, suggest that they sing it to themselves.

Make copies of your poster on colored paper. Give them to schools, libraries, police and fire departments, and families with young children in your community.

Help Clean Up Graffiti

In many cities and communities, graffiti is becoming an increasing problem. Walls, office buildings, homes, and store signs are often defaced with spray paint.

Volunteer your services to help clean up graffiti in your community. Get a group of your friends to help. Also solicit the help of parents and other adults to clean up graffiti you can't reach. Get permission from the owner of the property before you begin.

Some graffiti can be removed with commercial cleaning solutions. Other surfaces will need to be repainted. Ask local stores to donate the needed supplies.

Plan a clean-up day. Sign up volunteers in advance, and provide refreshments for everyone who helps.

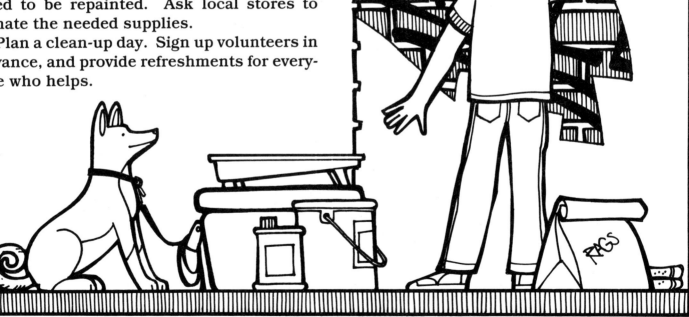

Write to a Newspaper

A good way to let a lot of people know about a concern in your community is to write a letter to your local newspaper. Respond to something you've read about or seen that needs attention. Let the paper know your opinion, and suggest ways to improve or address the situation. Send your letter to the editor of the paper. The editor's name and the address of the paper are usually printed in the newspaper, often on the page where letters to the editor appear.

Check your letter to make sure your ideas are clear and that each word is spelled correctly. Sign the letter and include your age.

Make a Community Activities Guide

Make a community activities guide of interesting and fun things for families or individuals to do in your community. Check with your local museum, tourist office, and library for ideas and information brochures.

Organize sections of your guide for different age groups, locations, and costs. Be sure to include lots of activities that are free or inexpensive. Share your guide by making copies for your school, library, or a community facility.

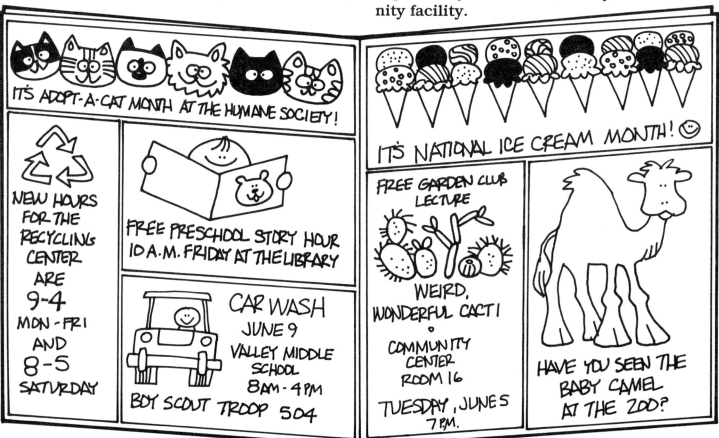

Volunteer in an Election

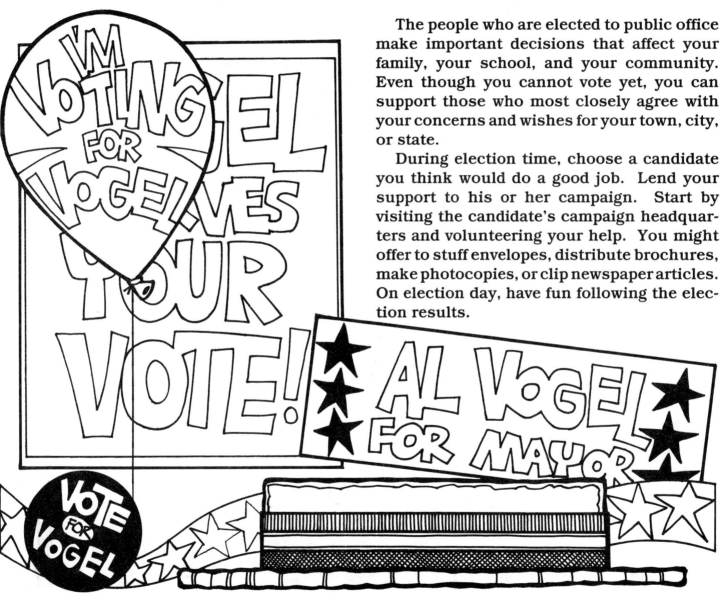

The people who are elected to public office make important decisions that affect your family, your school, and your community. Even though you cannot vote yet, you can support those who most closely agree with your concerns and wishes for your town, city, or state.

During election time, choose a candidate you think would do a good job. Lend your support to his or her campaign. Start by visiting the candidate's campaign headquarters and volunteering your help. You might offer to stuff envelopes, distribute brochures, make photocopies, or clip newspaper articles. On election day, have fun following the election results.

Pick a Park

Pick a park in your neighborhood or community, and volunteer to clean the area once a month for a year. Before beginning work on this project, get permission from the proper sources, such as someone who works for the city or county parks department. Get a group of your friends and classmates to help you with this project. Set goals for your group each time you get together. For example, you can have contests to see who can bag the most litter or who can find and recycle the most aluminum cans. Be sure to wear protective gloves when you pick up trash.

If there isn't a park in your community, pick any area such as a beach, a greenbelt, or an empty lot that needs attention, and volunteer to keep it clean.

Kids Who Care

Stephanie Wolf is 10 years old and is in the fourth grade at Mountain View Elementary School in Santa Barbara, California.

Stephanie decided to combine her love of journalism and computers to publish a newsletter for her neighborhood. Her first newsletter was three pages long and included national and local news as well as an interview with a neighbor, want ads, art work, interesting facts about people and animals, and other feature articles. Stephanie has recently invited some friends to join her staff and has plans to expand her publication, called *Neighborhood Newsletter*, to six pages.

Stephanie distributes her newsletter free of charge and has gotten positive feedback for her endeavors. She also has gained valuable experience in conducting interviews, writing articles, and publishing and printing a newsletter—a great start for a future journalist.

Matt (age 13), Grady (age 11), and Jeff Wheeler (age 8) are brothers who live in Garland, Texas. The boys have helped their community by working with others to build a house for people who could not afford to buy one.

They worked with an organization called Habitat for Humanity. Habitat provides volunteers to help build houses for people who can't afford to pay for the construction. The Wheeler brothers helped clean up and haul away trash at the construction site, helped build porches, and painted. They learned new skills, and they also got to meet the people they were helping—the family that moved into the house when it was finished.

The boys all help in other ways, too. Matt picks up litter regularly with his church youth group. Grady visits a nursing home to provide friendship for the elderly people who live there. Jeff sold tickets to a show that raised money for Boy Scout activities.

Community Organizations

Since organizations vary from community to community, it is not possible to list names and addresses that will apply to every location. In many cities, however, there is a listing of community services in the front of the local telephone directory under city government offices.

The names and addresses of several national organizations are listed below. Check your local telephone directory to see if there is an office in your area. If there isn't, contact the central office for the nearest location.

American National Red Cross
17th and D Streets, N.W.
Washington, D.C. 20006

CARE
151 Ellis Street
Atlanta, GA 30303

Children's Quilt Project
1478 University Avenue, Suite 186
Berkeley, CA 94702

Goodwill Industries of America, Inc.
9200 Wisconsin Avenue
Bethesda, MD 20814

The Salvation Army
National Headquarters
P.O. Box 269
Alexandria, VA 22313

Special Olympics International
1350 New York Avenue, Suite 500 N.W.
Washington, D.C. 20005

United Way of America
1701 North Fairfax Street
Alexandria, VA 22314

Volunteers of America
3813 North Causeway Boulevard
Metairie, LA 70002

Youth Services of America
1319 F Street N.W., Suite 900
Washington, D.C. 20004

Helping the Environment

Plan an Aluminum Can Drive

Organize a drive at your school to collect and recycle aluminum cans. Get your classmates to help.

Plan your drive with the following questions in mind: When and where will it be held? Which adults can help? Who will provide containers to hold the cans you collect? Who will take these cans to a recycling center?

With the help of a teacher or principal, schedule dates for your aluminum can drive. Designate a place on the school grounds or in your school parking lot as the official collection site.

Contact a recycling center that handles aluminum and find out its hours of operation. Ask the center personnel for tips about how to prepare the aluminum cans for recycling. The center may also have large containers you can borrow for your aluminum can drive.

COLLECT ALL THE CANS YOU CAN AND SUPPORT THE MILLER MIDDLE SCHOOL ALUMINUM CAN DRIVE NOVEMBER 1-18

Plan an Aluminum Can Drive
(continued)

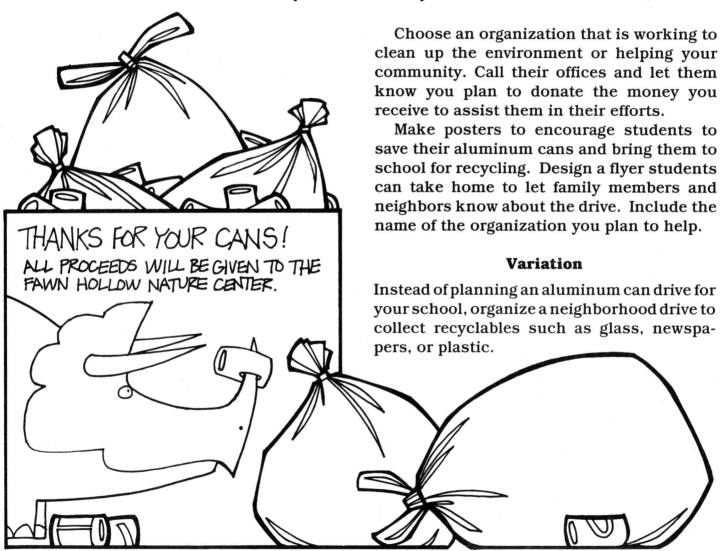

THANKS FOR YOUR CANS!

ALL PROCEEDS WILL BE GIVEN TO THE FAWN HOLLOW NATURE CENTER.

Choose an organization that is working to clean up the environment or helping your community. Call their offices and let them know you plan to donate the money you receive to assist them in their efforts.

Make posters to encourage students to save their aluminum cans and bring them to school for recycling. Design a flyer students can take home to let family members and neighbors know about the drive. Include the name of the organization you plan to help.

Variation

Instead of planning an aluminum can drive for your school, organize a neighborhood drive to collect recyclables such as glass, newspapers, or plastic.

Organize a Treasure Hunt

With a group of friends, conduct a clean-up treasure hunt on your school grounds. Not only will you have fun looking for the items listed, but you will be picking up litter and recycling, two activities that go a long way in creating a cleaner environment.

WHAT YOU NEED

- a group of friends to divide into teams
- two trash bags for each team
- gloves to protect participants' hands
- five sturdy boxes labeled **glass**, **metal**, **paper**, **plastic**, and **organic**
- at least one copy of the "Wanted List" for each team (see sample at right)
- pencils (to check off items on the list)

Wanted List

- ❑ a ballpoint pen
- ❑ a bottle cap
- ❑ a broken crayon
- ❑ a candy wrapper
- ❑ a lunch bag
- ❑ a paper clip
- ❑ a pencil
- ❑ a piece of clothing
- ❑ notebook paper
- ❑ a rubber band
- ❑ a green object
- ❑ a blue object
- ❑ a red object
- ❑ a yellow object
- ❑ something glass
- ❑ something metal
- ❑ something plastic
- ❑ something round
- ❑ something square
- ❑ a leaf or twig

> We abuse land because we regard it as a commodity belonging to us. When we see land as a community to which we belong, we may begin to use it with love and respect.
> —*Aldo Leopold*

Organize a Treasure Hunt
(continued)

WHAT YOU DO

- Divide the group into teams of two or more.

- Give each team two trash bags, gloves, and a copy of the "Wanted List" on page 104.

- Set a time limit.

- Spread out and search for the items listed.

- As you find the items, check them off the list.

- Carefully pick up the items and place them into one of the trash bags.

- Use the second trash bag for items that are not on your list.

- When the time is up, see which team has found the most listed items and declare this team the winner.

- Sort all of the litter into the labeled boxes.

- Dispose of the litter properly. Reuse or recycle what you can. Discard the rest by placing it in a school garbage can or trash bin.

Adopt a Stream

With a group of friends or classmates, adopt a stream in your community. Take steps to protect it from pollution. For example, you might pick up litter alongside the stream so that it will not fall into the water. You might also look for possible sources of pollution, and report any you find to adults who can decide what should be done. Be sure that the stream is located on public property and that you are not trespassing on private property. For more information, write to:

Save Our Streams
The Izaak Walton League of America
1401 Wilson Boulevard
Level B
Arlington, Virginia 22209

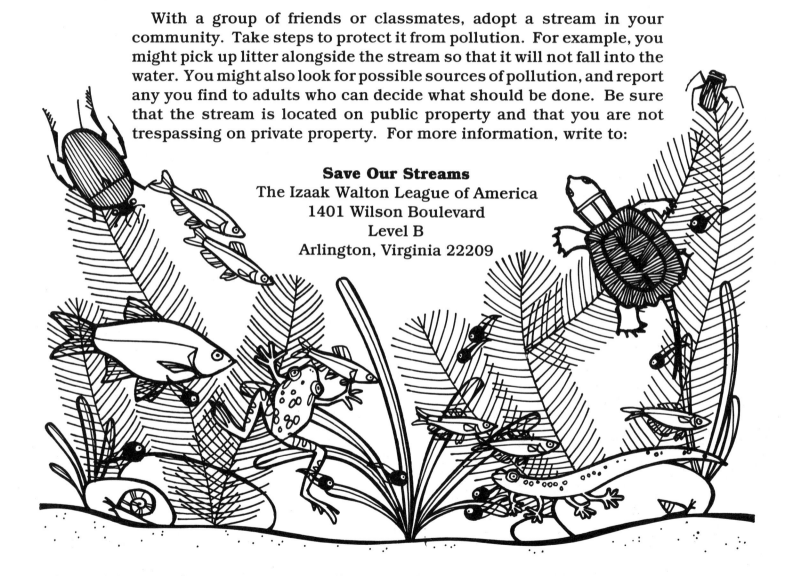

Plant a Tree

Trees are vital to our environment. They provide fruit and nuts to eat and are home and shelter to many animals. Trees also clean and renew the earth's atmosphere by producing oxygen. They provide shade and add beauty to our world.

Help the environment by planning a tree-planting party with your friends, classmates, neighbors, or scout troop. Start by talking to someone at your local nursery to learn more about what kinds of trees grow best in your area. Then get your group together and decide on the best place to plant your tree. Ask the people at the nursery to give you tips on the best way to plant and care for the tree you have selected. If you tell the nursery manager what you plan to do with your tree, perhaps he or she will contribute a sapling for your project. Also plan a schedule for the maintenance of your tree. Make your tree planting a special occasion by planning a dedication ceremony. Invite business leaders and governmental officials in your community to participate in the ceremony and to join in the festivities.

Enjoy the tree you planted and know that your gift will provide benefits to the environment for many years to come.

Never say there is nothing beautiful in the world any more. There is always something to make you wonder in the shape of a tree, the trembling of a leaf.

—*Albert Schweitzer*

Design a Trash Sculpture

Here's a fun way to promote the importance of reusing and recycling trash. This project also makes people more aware of how much trash they create on a daily basis.

Make a trash sculpture to display at your school, the public library, or another public place in your community where people can view it and learn more about recycling.

Start by collecting egg cartons, foam cups, paper plates, junk mail, plastic bottles and eating utensils, drinking straws, magazines, newspapers, and other trash. Then use staples, tape, or quick-drying glue to put these pieces of trash together into a sculpture. To give your sculpture a finished look, mount it on a cardboard base or box lid. Give your recycled trash sculpture a title.

Collect facts about recycling and the effects of trash on the environment. Make a poster of these facts to display with your sculpture.

Winning the environmental war is a whole lot tougher challenge by far than winning any other war in the history of man.
—*Gaylord Nelson*

Make a Banner

Design an environmental banner that shows people how you feel about the environment. Your theme can be conserving natural resources, cleaning up litter, protecting endangered animals, saving energy, stopping deforestation, or other environmental issues you feel strongly about.

Draw your design on a piece of paper. Use crayons or felt-tipped pens to color it. You can also make a banner using felt and hang it from a dowel. Another idea is to create a banner from an old bedsheet and use masking tape to attach it to a broomstick or pole.

Let us permit Nature to have her way; she understands her business better than we do.

—*Michel de Montaigne*

Publish a Newsletter

One way to make people aware of your environmental concerns is to publish a newsletter about them. You can create your newsletter on a computer or on a typewriter. Your newsletter can then be copied and distributed to others to read.

Think of a name for your newsletter. This name should be no longer than two or three words and should tell people what the newsletter is about. Use one of the following names or create your own.

The Planet Protector
The Earth Times
Earth Chronicle
Wildlife Watch
The Weekly Wave
Global Concern
Nature News

Display this name in the nameplate at the top of the front page of your newsletter. Below the name, print a line showing the issue number and date of your newsletter as shown in the example at right.

Publish a Newsletter
(continued)

Publishing a newsletter involves a lot of work, so ask friends and classmates to become members of your newsletter staff. Be sure to give credit to the people who have helped you by listing their names and titles in your newsletter.

Discuss the purpose of the newsletter with members of your staff. Decide what topics you will cover and how you will treat these topics. Will you give the facts in a news story, give opinions in an editorial, or write a feature story to inform and entertain your readers?

Talk about your editorial policy. Establish guidelines and set reasonable deadlines for the newsletter. Discuss how you will distribute the newsletter to family, friends, and neighbors.

To make your newsletter more interesting, plan to include special features such as cartoons, drawings, riddles, games, little-known facts, crossword puzzles, an ask-the-expert column, and letters to the editor.

Create an Energy Contract

Think of three things you can do each day to conserve energy during a two-week period. Then, write an energy contract in which you promise to save energy by doing these three things. In writing the contract, follow the example shown on page 113 or create your own contract. Ask mom or dad to sign your contract, and then do what you promised.

At the end of two weeks, evaluate your results. Were you successful in meeting the energy-saving goals you set for yourself? What difficulties did you encounter? See if you can make these three energy-saving ideas and others like them a regular part of your own earth-friendly life-style.

Ask members of your family to create energy contracts as well. You can also make this a school project in which all of your classmates work to save energy in their homes and at school.

Create an Energy Contract
(continued)

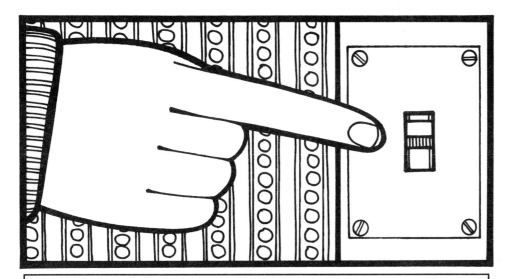

Energy Contract

I, _____,
promise that I shall help
to conserve energy for a
period of two weeks by:

1. _____

_____

2. _____

_____

3. _____

_____

_____
signature

_____
date

_____
parent's signature

Ideas

- Turn off the lights when you are the last person to walk out of a room.

- Install a water-saving showerhead and take shorter showers.

- Walk or ride a bicycle to school instead of being driven in a car.

- If you can't walk or ride a bicycle to school, join a carpool or take a bus.

- Use manual pencil sharpeners and can openers instead of electric ones.

Decorate a Recycled Box

Here's a fun project you can do by yourself or with a group of friends. Decorate an empty cereal box to hold sheets of paper that have been used on one side but are still clean on the other side.

WHAT YOU NEED

- a large cereal box
- recycled gift wrap or brown paper cut from a grocery sack
- felt-tipped pens
- scissors
- tape
- glue

WHAT YOU DO

1. Cover the box with the paper and tape the ends in place.

2. Label the box by cutting letters from paper scraps and gluing them to the box or by writing on the box with felt-tipped pens.

3. Decorate the box by drawing on it and/or by gluing paper shapes to it.

4. Use the box to hold copier paper, computer paper, or writing paper that has been used only on one side.

5. Donate your decorated boxes to teachers in your school or to businesses in your community.

Man shapes himself through decisions that shape his environment.
—René Dubos

Help Save a Rain Forest

Tropical rain forests swarm with life. Bright-colored frogs, speckled salamanders, and huge beetles putter among the trees. Snakes glide silently along hanging vines while parrots scream overhead. Hummingbirds dart among the flowers. In the distance, a jaguar roars.

At least half of the world's species of animals and plants are found in the rain forest. Most cannot exist anywhere else.

Unfortunately, thousands of acres of rain forest are being destroyed *every day*, as trees are cut for lumber and the land is cleared for agricultural use. Without trees to protect it from heavy rainfall, the soil washes away. Soon the land is bare and useless. As a result of rain forest destruction, thousands of species of animals and plants are becoming extinct each year.

How can you help? Many organizations are working to save rain forests. One is The Nature Conservancy (see address, page 118) which has an "adopt-an-acre" rain forest program. By donating money, you can help them purchase and protect rain forest land. Write to them for more information. Some ideas for how to earn money are listed on pages 120–144 of this book.

I hope to be remembered as someone who made the earth a little more beautiful.
—*Justice William O. Douglas*

Kids Who Care

Every fourth grader in Tennessee is a kid who cares for the environment!

Since 1990, the Division of Forestry and several other organizations have sponsored a program called Tennessee Releaf. The Division of Forestry distributes tulip poplar seedlings to fourth graders throughout the state on Tennessee Arbor Day. The kids plant the trees—as many as 40,000 a year.

Trees can make a big difference for the environment. Dwight Barnett, a staff forester who is involved with Tennessee Releaf, says that planting one shade tree on the southwest side of a house can cut the cost of air-conditioning the house by 50 percent.

Melissa Poe was nine years old when she saw a television program that scared her. It showed what our environment would be like in the future if people kept polluting it. Melissa decided to do something to get more people to help the environment. She wrote a letter to George Bush, former president of the United States, asking him to put up signs telling people to stop polluting. She thought that people would listen to the president. But he didn't answer her letter. So Melissa decided to put up signs herself. She put her letter to the president on a billboard. With the help of advertising agencies, Melissa continued to put up billboards, until her letter appeared on 250 of them.

Melissa also started an organization called KidsF.A.C.E.™ (Kids for a Clean Environment). Today KidsF.A.C.E.™ has 200,000 members in the United States and in other countries. One KidsF.A.C.E.™ project is called School of Trees. It teaches kids how to create habitats for wildlife in their backyards.

Environmental Organizations

Acid Rain Foundation, Inc.
1410 Varsity Drive
Raleigh, NC 27606

America the Beautiful Fund
219 Shoreham Building
Washington, D.C. 20005

American Forestry Association
Global ReLeaf
P.O. Box 2000
Washington, D.C. 20010

American Water Works Association
6666 W. Quincy Avenue
Denver, CO 80235
Attention: Student Programs Manager

Citizens for a Better Environment
924 Market Street, Suite 505
San Francisco, CA 94102

The Cousteau Society
8440 Santa Monica Blvd.
Los Angeles, CA 90069

Earth Birthday Project
183 Pinehurst, #34
New York, NY 10033

Environmental Action Coalition
625 Broadway, 2nd Floor
New York, NY 10012

Environmental Defense Fund
257 Park Avenue, South
New York, NY 10010

Environmental Hazards Management
Institute (EHMI)
P.O. Box 932
10 Newmarket Road
Durham, NH 03824

Friends of the Earth
218 D Street, S.E.
Washington, D.C. 20013

Greenpeace
1611 Connecticut Avenue N.W.
Washington, D.C. 20016

Environmental Organizations
(continued)

The Institute for Earth Education
Cedar Cove
Greenville, WV 24945–0115

Keep America Beautiful, Inc.
9 W. Broad Street
Stamford, CT 06902

National Arbor Day Foundation
100 Arbor Avenue
Nebraska City, NE 68410

National Recycling Coalition
1101 30th Street, N.W., Suite 305
Washington, D.C. 20007

The Natural Resources Defense Council
40 W. 20th Street
New York, NY 10011

The Nature Conservancy
1815 N. Lynn Street
Arlington, VA 22209

The New Alchemy Institute
237 Hatchville Road
East Falmouth, MA 02536

Sierra Club
730 Polk Street
San Francisco, CA 94109

Trees for Life
1103 Jefferson
Wichita, KS 67203

U.S. Environmental Protection Agency (EPA)
401 M Street S.W.
A 108
Washington, D.C. 20460

Western Regional Environmental Education Council
2820 Echo Way
Sacramento, CA 95821

Fund-Raising Ideas

Introduction

Many high school students hold part-time jobs or receive money from allowances that they can donate to worthwhile causes. For kids under age 16, however, it can be very difficult to find a job. The purpose of this section is to present ideas for services you can provide and items you can make and sell to raise money for charitable causes. Several methods for advertising your service or product are also covered.

When raising money to donate to charitable organizations, it is important to know and understand the various legal steps you need to take and the laws you must follow.

This section covers:

- how to apply for a Social Security number

- sales tax and income tax

- how to obtain a sales permit

Erin's Errands
RATES
25¢ PER BLOCK
PLUS
4¢ PER MINUTE
(STARTING AT MY HOUSE)

CRITTER SITTING PRICE PER DAY

MOUSE OR HAMSTER	.35
RAT OR PARAKEET	.50
GUINEA PIG OR RABBIT	1.00
FISH (PER AQUARIUM)	.35
CAT OR SMALL DOG	2.00
MEDIUM DOG	3.00
LARGE DOG	5.00

PETRIFIED FRIENDS

ANIMAL STONE PAINTINGS $2.00 SMALL • $3.00 LARGE

Applying for a Social Security Number

The law now requires everyone five years of age and older to have a Social Security number. There is no charge for getting a Social Security card. The card has a special number that is issued by the Social Security Administration. This is an identification number you will keep throughout your life, present when you apply for jobs, and use later on when you file income tax returns.

When you work, a certain part of your income is paid into a special account. Then, when you reach retirement age (usually in your sixties), you can apply to draw on the money that has been put aside. After you retire, you receive a monthly Social Security check. How much money you receive each month depends on how much you earned while paying into the account.

Ask your mom or dad if you have already been issued a Social Security number. If not, you can find information about getting a Social Security number from the United States Social Security Administration. Their phone number is located under "United States Government," a listing commonly found in the front of the phone book. Once you have found the heading, look under "S" for Social Security Administration. Call their office and ask them to send you the necessary paperwork to apply for your Social Security number. Fill out the form, sign your name, and return the form to your local Social Security office. Along with the completed form, you must send in your original birth certificate or a certified copy, which will be returned to you. Your Social Security card will then be sent to you.

777-90-2325
SOCIAL SECURITY ACCOUNT NUMBER

Elisa Estrella
2415 Aster Avenue
Portland, OR 97203

SIGNATURE *Elisa Estrella*
FOR SOCIAL SECURITY & TAX PURPOSES · NOT FOR I.D.

Taxes, Laws, and Permits

Sales Tax

If you plan to sell something, check with the Small Business Administration office in your area to see if you have to pay state or city sales tax. If you do, this tax is passed on to your customers and added to the cost of the item.

Sales Permits

Sometimes, local laws require you to obtain a sales permit when you sell door to door or from a stand on your street corner. Check with the Small Business Administration office listed in your telephone book.

Income Tax

Check with the Internal Revenue Service to find out if you are required to file an income tax form at the end of the year for monies you have raised. Their toll-free telephone number is 800-829-1040.

Food Laws

If your fund-raiser involves preparing and selling food, check with your local county health department to see what rules apply. In order to protect the public, the government has established strict rules regarding the preparation and handling of food being sold. Other agencies that can provide you with information include the United States Food and Drug Administration and the Small Business Administration.

Advertising Your Product or Service

Advertising is a way of letting people know about the product or service you have to offer. Advertising can take several forms.

Signs and posters

Make signs or posters and display them on bulletin boards, in store windows, in supermarkets, and in libraries. Be sure to get permission before posting your signs. Take the signs down when they are no longer needed.

Flyers

Design a flyer describing important information about your product or service. Use illustrations to make your flyer attractive and fun to read. Be sure to include your name and phone number. Make multiple copies of your flyer at a copy shop. Distribute your flyers to neighbors, friends, and relatives.

Newspaper ads

Advertise in the classified section of your local newspaper. Keep the ad short as the cost of the ad usually depends on the number of words used. For information on prices and deadlines, call the newspaper's offices and ask to speak to someone who sells classified advertising.

Advertising Your Product or Service
(continued)

Door to Door

Go door to door telling people about your product or service. Keep your sales pitch short and to the point. Only visit neighborhoods you are familiar with, and don't go inside the house when you make your sales pitch. Speak slowly and clearly, and leave a business card or flyer so potential customers can contact you.

Word of Mouth

This kind of advertising doesn't cost you anything but is extremely effective. When you satisfy customers by providing exceptional service, fair prices, and quality products, they will tell other people. This word-of-mouth advertising will bring in more customers.

Organizing a Recipe File

People often have recipes they've gathered over the years from magazines, newspapers, family, and friends. Many times these recipes are thrown in a drawer or tossed into a box. To earn money for your special cause, become a recipe file organizer.

WHAT YOU NEED

- your customer's recipes
- large envelopes
- 4" x 6" index cards
- 4" x 6" divider cards
- a file box for the index cards
- a pen, computer, or typewriter
- clear tape

WHAT YOU DO

1. Take the recipes and organize them by food categories. Separate them into envelopes marked as follows:

- appetizers
- soups
- salads
- casseroles
- poultry dishes
- meat dishes
- seafood dishes
- desserts
- beverages
- miscellaneous

2. Print or type the recipes on the index cards. Check to be sure you have copied everything correctly. You can also tape shorter recipes to the index cards.

3. Arrange the index cards in the file box by category and alphabetize them. Put a labeled divider card at the beginning of each category.

4. Design a label like the one shown to put on the outside of the recipe file.

> **IMA BAKER'S FAVORITE RECIPES**
> *Compiled by Itoko Taguchi*

House-Sitting

When people go on vacation, they often need someone to take care of their house or apartment. Here are some things you can do to raise money as a house-sitter.

Bring mail, packages, and newspapers inside. Water house plants.

Adjust blinds, drapes, and window shades daily so the home looks lived in.

Turn inside lights on in the evening, varying the lights in different rooms each night.

- Make sure you have a name, address, and phone number where the homeowner can be reached in case of an emergency.

- Be sure to lock the house securely when you leave. Check the door to make sure it is properly locked. Put the key in a safe place in your home.

- See page 128 for ideas on taking care of people's pets while they are on vacation.

WATER PLANT EVERY OTHER DAY.

Calligraphy

If you have good penmanship and enjoy writing, you can raise money by designing invitations and announcements. Special calligraphy pen sets are available at office supply, art, and stationery stores. Check to see if a calligraphy class is offered at your school or a local community center. Practice until you perfect your calligraphy. Make sure to have your customer approve a sample of your work before completing the entire job.

Some of the items you might consider designing are:

PLACE CARDS

INVITATIONS

ANNOUNCEMENTS

Critter Sitting

When people go on vacation, you can
earn money by taking care of their pets.

You can help by

providing food and water,

*exercising and grooming
the animals,*

and keeping pet areas clean.

- Ask the family to leave a telephone number where
  they can be reached in case of an emergency.

- Keep the name, address, and telephone number of
  their veterinarian handy, and know the location of
  the nearest 24-hour animal care center.

RAMONA RAT
DAILY
· CHECK FOOD AND WATER
· GIVE TREATS: 1 RAISIN, ½ PEANUT.
· ___ ITH HER - SHE LIKES TO
  ___ ON YOUR SHOULDER
  ___EKLY
  ___EAN CAGE (SHAVINGS ARE ON
  ___ORCH NEXT TO CAT FOOD).

Window Washing

Raise money by cleaning the windows
of single-story homes and businesses.

WHAT YOU NEED

- commercial glass cleaner or a mixture of ammonia and warm water
- plenty of lint-free rags
- newspapers
- a bucket
- sponges
- a squeegee
- a stepladder
- a plastic drop cloth

WHAT YOU DO

1. Use commercial glass cleaner or make your own. Mix ammonia with warm water and pour the mixture into a spray bottle.*

2. If necessary, prepare the area where you are going to work by moving furniture and spreading a plastic drop cloth to protect the floor or carpeting.

3. Spray the cleaner on the inside surface of the window. Use newspapers or lint-free rags to wipe them dry. Repeat on the outside surface.

4. For larger windows, use a bucket of water and ammonia instead of the spray bottle. Sponge on the cleaner, and use a squeegee to dry it.

5. Check your work to make sure there are no streaks or places you missed.

* Generally, you can add one-half cup of ammonia to one gallon of warm water, but follow the directions on the product you are using. You may wish to protect your hands with vinyl or rubber gloves.

Cupboard Cleaning

Many people don't make time in their busy schedules to clean out their kitchen cupboards, pantries, and drawers. Here's an idea that could bring you lots of interested customers.

WHAT YOU NEED

- bucket of warm water
- damp sponge
- dry cloth

WHAT YOU DO

1. Remove the items from one shelf or drawer at a time to be sure things go back where they belong.

2. Using a damp sponge, wipe the empty areas thoroughly.

3. Dry the shelves and drawers before putting the items back in place.

4. In the pantry, separate canned fruits from canned vegetables. Arrange boxes according to categories such as cereals, spices, pastas, etc.

5. If a customer wants to supply shelf paper, you can also line shelves and drawers.

Gardening

Caring for the yards and gardens of neighbors, friends, and family is a practical way to raise money. Before you start, make sure to learn about the safe use of garden tools and equipment such as mowers, pruning shears, and hedge trimmers.

Gardening Services You Can Offer:

- fertilize lawns
- mow and water lawns
- pick up trash
- plant flowers
- rake leaves and trimmings
- trim bushes and shrubs
- weed lawns and gardens

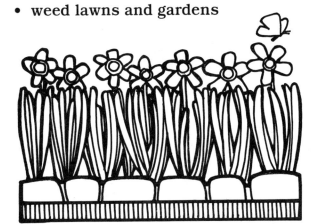

Fill out a worksheet for each customer using the sample below.

PAT'S GARDENING WORKSHEET

Customer's name _____

Address_____

Phone _____

Schedule (circle one)

   Mon. Tues. Wed. Thur. Fri. Sat. Sun.

Time _____ How often? _____

Special notes _____

_____

Children's Party Assistant

If you enjoy working with younger children, consider raising
money by offering your services as a children's party helper.

You can help by

decorating,

organizing games,

serving refreshments,

and cleaning up.

- Go over the details of the party with the child's parents. Ask about the number of guests, their ages, and the time of the party.

- Plan games that are appropriate for the age group attending the party. Your local library has books that are filled with game and party ideas if you need help.

- Make a list of the gifts received and who sent them so that the host or hostess can send thank-you notes.

Party Assistant

Planning and giving parties can be a lot of work. There are many things you can do to help the host or hostess before, during, and after a party. Here are ideas for ways to earn money as a party assistant.

BEFORE

- address invitations
- decorate the house
- set up tables and chairs
- dust, vacuum, clean mirrors
- arrange centerpieces
- set the tables
- make hors d'oeuvres
- help prepare the food

DURING

- help serve the food
- replenish food on the party platters
- make and serve coffee and tea
- clear away used dishes
- wash pots and pans

AFTER

- wash, dry, and put dishes away
- wrap up leftovers
- remove tables and chairs
- clean the kitchen and party area
- take out the garbage
- mop the floor

Magician

Visit your public or school library and find books that describe simple magic tricks you can perform. Practice these tricks in front of friends and family until you can perform them with ease and confidence. Then plan a magic show for younger children, or offer to perform at a birthday party.

Many young children cannot sit still for very long, so plan to make your show last about 20 minutes. Call on kids in the audience to pick a card, hold a scarf for one of your tricks, or guess which box a peanut is under. Make them feel like they are part of your magic show.

Charge admission and donate the money to your favorite charity or organization.

Computer Whiz

If you have a computer and have a knack for design, there are many ways you can raise money by creating printed materials. Start by making a notebook with samples of your work. Your notebook can include any of the following:

- announcements
- banners
- brochures
- business cards
- flyers

- greeting cards
- invitations
- menus
- place cards
- signs

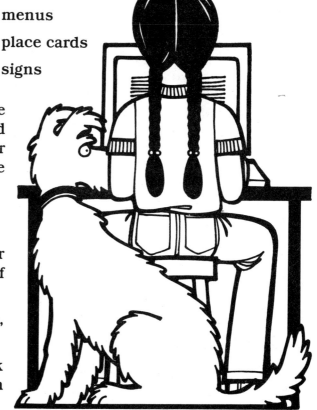

Find customers by showing your notebook to store owners, businesspeople, secretaries, teachers, and people involved with nonprofit organizations in your community. Let them know that you are donating the money you earn to a worthwhile cause.

Helpful Hints

- Ask your clients about deadlines, and do your best to meet them. Let them know in advance if you need more time.

- Carefully check your work for errors. If possible, have another person proofread your work.

- Provide a sample, or *proof*, of the job and ask your client to sign an approval before you run multiple copies.

Baby-Sitting

Baby-sitting can provide a means of raising money for an organization of your choice. Let your customers know that you are donating the money you earn, and tell them something about the special cause you are contributing to.

Helpful Hints

- Arrive a few minutes early so you can talk with the parents about special instructions.

- If this is the first time you are baby-sitting for the family, ask the parents to fill out an information card (in pencil) like the one below before they leave. Bring the card each time you baby-sit for the family. Be sure to update the phone number where the parents can be reached.

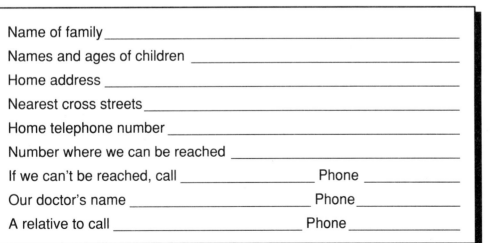

Name of family _____

Names and ages of children _____

Home address _____

Nearest cross streets _____

Home telephone number _____

Number where we can be reached _____

If we can't be reached, call _____ Phone _____

Our doctor's name _____ Phone _____

A relative to call _____ Phone _____

Baby-Sitting
(continued)

Helpful Hints

- Bring a tote bag filled with fun things to do that are appropriate to the ages of the children you are caring for. For example, you might bring along a book to read, a puzzle, crayons and paper for drawing, or a favorite board game to play.

- Never leave young children alone or unattended, even for a minute.

- Spend time playing with the children, and get them to bed on time. Check on the children periodically after they have gone to bed.

Call Betsy Wall about the bake sale Saturday.
213·0412

- If someone calls, get a name and a telephone number so the child's parents can return the call. Do not tell the caller you are home alone with the children. Simply say that the parents can't come to the phone and you will be glad to take a message. Don't have your friends over or tie up the telephone with personal calls while baby-sitting.

- Put toys away and tidy the kids' play area so the house is neat when the parents return.

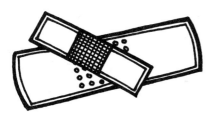

- Become familiar with safety rules, basic first aid, and emergency procedures. Special classes are offered for baby-sitters. Contact a local hospital or chapter of the American Red Cross, and sign up if these courses are offered.

Dog Walking

Many dog owners don't have sufficient time to exercise their pets. A dog walking service is a great way to raise money, keep yourself in shape, and make many canine friends.

Helpful Hints

- Ask the owner to provide you with a leash the dog is familiar with. Make sure the leash is comfortable and easy for you to hold.

- Find out about leash laws and city ordinances by calling your local Humane Society or Animal Control Department. Also ask these experts for tips on handling stubborn dogs and what to do in case of a runaway dog.

- Ask the owner if the dog has fears such as loud noises or bicycles, or any behavior problems the dog has that you should know about (such as chasing cats or cars, or jumping up on people).

- Keep the dog on the leash the entire time it is in your care, and keep a watchful eye on the dog at all times.

- Carry a plastic bag for picking up any messes the dog makes. Slip the bag over your hand and pick up the dog droppings. Then pull the bag off of your hand so that the droppings are inside it, tie it shut, and dispose of it in a trash can.

- Be kind to and patient with the pet in your care. Keep in mind that the dog's owner is trusting you with a special member of the family.

Bargain Book Sale

Get a group of friends together and raise money by asking neighbors, relatives, and friends to donate books for a "Bargain Book Sale." Display the books you collect in boxes that are clearly labeled by category. Put a price sticker in the upper corner of each book.

Helpful Hints

- Start by separating the books for children from the books for adults. In each category, separate the fiction from the nonfiction.

- Further separate the fiction books by categories such as romance, mystery, and science fiction. The nonfiction books can be separated into categories such as biographies, cookbooks, "how-to" books, crafts, and travel.

- Make signs for each category so your customers can find their favorite kinds of books.

- Provide recycled paper or plastic bags for your customers' purchases.

- Have fun making and selling bookmarks to go with the books. (See the directions on page 158.)

SUGGESTED PRICES

Children's books (small)	$.25
Children's picture books (large)	$.50–$1.00
Adult paperback books	$.35–$.50
Adult hardcover books	$1.00–$5.00
Magazines	$.25–$.75
Comic Books	$.25

Run Errands

Start an errand service in your neighborhood, and do all the small, day-to-day chores that people don't always have time to do.

Start by asking your family, relatives, and neighbors what types of daily chores they least like doing. Make a list of these jobs, and decide which ones are practical for you to do. (Consider the type of transportation that is available to you.)

Once you have decided on the kinds of errands you can offer, make a flyer describing these services. Distribute the flyer to your neighbors.

Here are some ideas of errands you can run for people:

- mailing letters
- returning books to the library
- picking up groceries
- picking up items at a drug store or pharmacy
- taking aluminum cans and newspapers to a recycling center
- making bank deposits

Garage Sale

To raise money, offer your services to a family that is planning a weekend garage sale. If your family has enough items to sell, plan your own garage sale. Here are some things you can do.

make posters and
flyers and put them up
prior to the sale

tag and price
sale items

set up tables
for display

arrange and
display items

help customers and
collect money

help clean up and
pack unsold items

take posters down
after the sale

donate unsold items
to a charity

Car Wash

Raise money by washing cars. Ask friends to join you to make the job go faster and to make it more fun.

TO CLEAN THE EXTERIOR

What You Need

- garden hose and water
- bucket
- sponges
- a mild liquid soap
- a stiff brush for cleaning tires
- clean rags or cloth towels (lint-free)
- glass cleaner
- paper towels

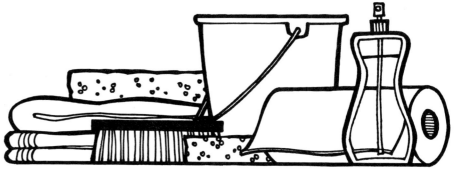

What You Do

1. Fill the bucket with water and soap.

2. Make sure the windows and doors are tightly closed. Hose the car with water.

3. Using a sponge, scrub the car, starting with the roof.

4. Rinse as you go. Do one section of the car at a time.

5. Scrub the tires with the brush.

6. Hose the car to remove all the soap.

7. Dry the car with the rags and towels.

8. Clean the inside and outside of the windows and the mirrors with glass cleaner and paper towels.

Helpful Hints

- Wash the car in the shade.

- Make sure the car is cool. A hot car will leave soap and water marks.

- Use a mild soap. Strong detergents can damage the paint.

Car Wash
(continued)

TO CLEAN THE INTERIOR

What You Need

- clean rags
- a portable or cordless vacuum cleaner
- spray cleaner for vinyl
- sponges
- a bucket of soapy water
- glass cleaner
- paper towels

What You Do

1. Remove the floor mats. Vacuum them if they are cloth. If they are rubber, scrub them with soap and water, rinse them, and allow them to dry.

2. Empty all the ashtrays. Clean them with a damp rag.

3. Clean the inside windows and mirrors with glass cleaner and paper towels.

4. Clean all the vinyl with spray. Follow the directions on the can or bottle.

5. Vacuum fabric seats, upholstery, and carpets.

Helpful Hints

- Turn off the car's ceiling light to spare the battery since the doors will be open as you work.

- Don't forget to replace the floor mats.

- To add a nice finishing touch, leave a litter bag in the car.

Gift Wrapping

Offer a gift wrapping service at holiday times for neighbors and family. This is a great project to do with a group of your friends. Most people will appreciate not having to wait in long lines during the busy holiday season.

What You Need

- wrapping paper
- ribbons
- clear tape
- scissors
- boxes of assorted sizes
- gift cards
- tissue paper
- ready-made bows

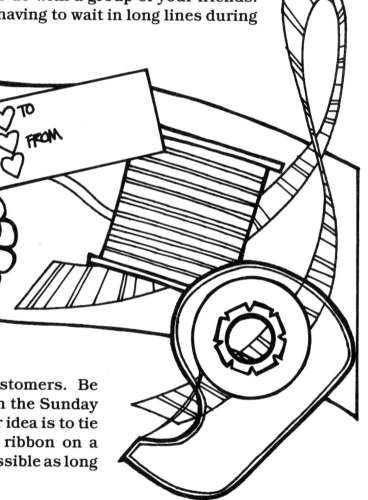

Helpful Hint

Make up sample packages to show your customers. Be creative! For example, a child's gift wrapped in the Sunday comic strips is festive and fun to read. Another idea is to tie an inexpensive rattle or teething ring to the ribbon on a baby's gift. Reuse wrapping paper whenever possible as long as it looks fresh and clean.

Gifts to Make for Others

Introduction

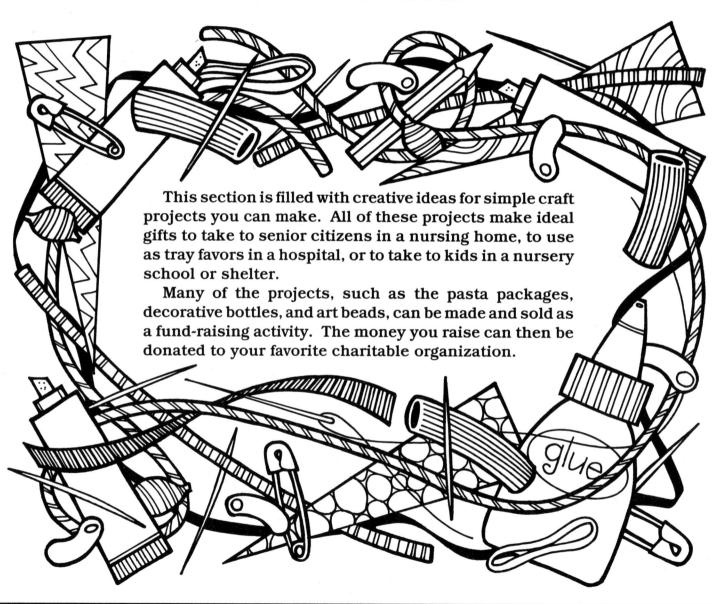

This section is filled with creative ideas for simple craft projects you can make. All of these projects make ideal gifts to take to senior citizens in a nursing home, to use as tray favors in a hospital, or to take to kids in a nursery school or shelter.

Many of the projects, such as the pasta packages, decorative bottles, and art beads, can be made and sold as a fund-raising activity. The money you raise can then be donated to your favorite charitable organization.

Terrific Name Tags

Make a colorful name tag to wear when you visit kids in a nursery school, shelter, or hospital.

WHAT YOU NEED

- ruler
- pencil
- white construction paper
- crayons or felt-tipped pens
- scissors
- safety pins

WHAT YOU DO

1. With a pencil and ruler, draw a three-inch square on the white paper.

2. Draw two or three lines across the top and bottom 1/4" apart.

3. Create a pattern within each row by repeating a shape like a triangle or star.

4. With a felt-tipped pen, carefully write your name in the center of the square. To help you keep the letters straight, use a ruler and pencil to lightly draw a guideline.

5. With crayons or pens, color the patterns you have created.

6. Cut out the finished tag, and pin it on so the kids can learn your name.

7. Now teach the kids how to make their own name tags. This will help you learn their names.

8. Don't forget to try this art activity with senior citizens, too!

Weave a Mat

Make a colorful placemat to brighten up a breakfast, lunch, or dinner tray for a child or adult in a hospital.

WHAT YOU NEED

- several sheets of 9" x 12" construction paper in assorted colors
- scissors
- ruler
- pencil
- glue

WHAT YOU DO

1. Fold one sheet of construction paper in half for your background. Draw a line one inch in from the edge opposite the folded side, as shown.

2. Draw straight or wavy lines from your folded edge to your one-inch line. Cut along these lines as shown.

3. Cut strips nine inches long and about one inch wide from the other sheets of construction paper.

4. Unfold your background sheet. Choose a strip to weave through the paper. Start on one side, and slide your paper strip *under* one background strip and *over* the next.

5. When you have woven the strip from one side to the other, push it toward the edge and make the ends even.

6. Do the same with the second strip, but this time go *over* and then *under*. Repeat these steps until your background space is full.

7. Trim the ends of your strips, and glue them down.

Pasta Packages

This container makes an ideal gift for kids and adults alike and will hold paper clips, rubber bands, jewelry, safety pins, or loose change.

WHAT YOU NEED

- a small box with a lid
- fancy dry pasta, such as bows, twists, and/or shells
- gold or silver spray paint
- ribbon, rick-rack, or yarn
- glue

WHAT YOU DO

1. Glue the pasta to the top of the lid.
2. Allow plenty of time for the glue to dry.
3. Spray both the container and the lid with gold or silver paint.
4. Glue ribbon, rick-rack, or yarn around the edge of the lid.

Caution

Spray paint can be both messy and dangerous. Before you use it, read the warnings on the label. Work in an area that is well ventilated. Spread out plenty of old newspapers to protect the floor and walls in this area. Shake the can well before spraying. Aim the nozzle carefully so that the paint will go where you want it to go and *not* toward your face or into your eyes.

Decorative Bottles

These gift bottles are ideal for use as pencil holders, vases, and desk organizers. Make them as gifts for someone who is sick at home or for a senior citizen.

WHAT YOU NEED

- old bottle or jar
- tissue paper in assorted colors
- scissors
- liquid starch
- shallow, wide-mouthed container (baby food jar or margarine tub)
- a paintbrush
- water-based clear shellac
- a wooden spoon
- a crockery or flower pot

Decorative Bottles
(continued)

WHAT YOU DO

1. Remove the label from the bottle or jar.

2. Cut the tissue paper into small pieces.

3. Pour the starch into the shallow container.

4. Place the handle of a wooden spoon inside your bottle. Place the spoon end into a crockery or flower pot. This will allow you to turn the bottle easily as you decorate it and will give the bottle a place to dry.

5. With one hand, hold a piece of tissue paper on the bottle. With the other hand, brush liquid starch over the tissue paper, onto the bottle. The starch will make the tissue stick to the bottle.

6. Continue adding pieces of tissue paper, until the bottle is completely covered.

7. Allow the starch to dry.

8. Clean out the paintbrush. Apply shellac to the bottle to make the surface shiny.

9. Allow the shellac to dry.

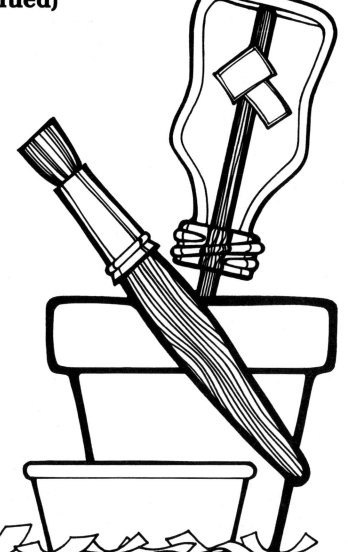

Art Beads

Bring this colorful necklace to a hospital patient, to a nursing home resident, or to a shelter to brighten someone's day.

WHAT YOU NEED

- a 2" x 5" piece of thin cardboard
- a pencil and a ruler
- a pair of scissors
- brightly colored pages torn from old magazines
- 12 round toothpicks or skewers
- white glue
- a needle with a large eye
- a spool of heavy thread

Art Beads
(continued)

WHAT YOU DO

1. Using the pencil and ruler, draw a triangle four inches wide and one and a half inches high (see drawing below) on a piece of cardboard or tagboard.

2. Cut out this triangle carefully so that the sides are straight and it can be used as a pattern.

3. Using this pattern, cut at least 12 triangles from the magazine pages.

4. Wrap the base of one triangle around a toothpick or skewer and roll it tightly.

5. Glue down the pointed end of the roll to hold it in place.

6. Repeat steps 4 and 5 until you have made about a dozen beads.

7. Allow the glue to dry.

8. Gently slide the beads off the toothpicks or skewers.

9. Using the needle, string the beads on a piece of heavy thread.

10. Knot both ends of the thread so that the beads will not slide off.

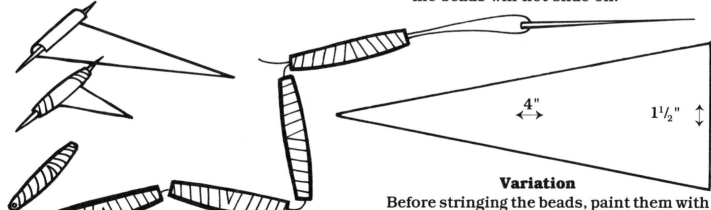

4"

1½"

Variation
Before stringing the beads, paint them with diluted white glue to harden the surface and make them shine.

Egg Cup Bouquets

Recycle empty egg cartons into fancy floral bouquets to brighten the tray of someone in a hospital or nursing home.

WHAT YOU NEED

- several egg cartons made of polystyrene foam in aqua, yellow, or some other pastel shade

- a pair of sharp scissors

- a sharpened pencil

- some pipe cleaners

- ribbon and/or a narrow-necked vase

Egg Cup Bouquets
(continued)

WHAT YOU DO

1. With scissors, cut the egg cartons into single egg cups.

2. To make these egg cups look like flowers, cut fringe, points, and scallops as shown.

3. Using the point of the pencil or scissors, carefully poke a small hole in the center of each egg cup.

4. Insert a pipe cleaner in the hole.

5. Bend the end of the pipe cleaner to hold it in place.

6. Tie the stems of your egg carton bouquet together with ribbon or place them in a narrow-necked vase.

Variation

Cut several egg cups to different heights and layer them together on the same pipe cleaner stem.

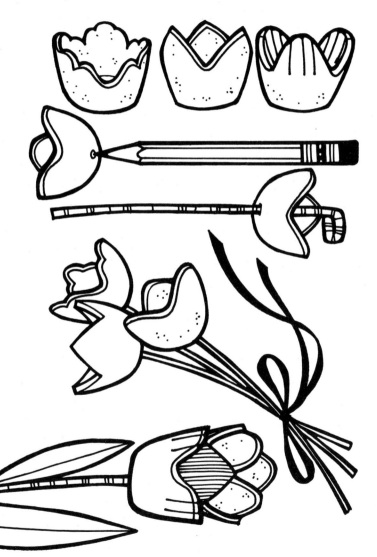

Can Creatures

Create an amazing array of creatures using lots of recycled cans and a little imagination. These containers make great gifts for people in hospitals and nursing homes. They are also fun for young kids to use to store crayons, school supplies, and collectibles.

WHAT YOU NEED

- empty cans in various shapes and sizes
- a roll of adhesive or masking tape
- a tape measure and a ruler
- a pencil
- some construction, shelf, or butcher paper
- scraps of paper and fabric
- a pair of scissors
- some tape or glue
- odds and ends, such as feathers, buttons, pipe cleaners, and ribbon, for decorating your creatures

Can Creatures
(continued)

WHAT YOU DO

1. Remove the paper label or wrapper from the can.

2. Wash and dry the can thoroughly.

3. If the top edges of the can are sharp or rough, carefully cover them with adhesive or masking tape so that you will not cut yourself when you handle the can.

4. Using the tape measure, measure around the can. Write down this measurement.

5. Using either the tape measure or the ruler, measure the can from top to bottom. Write down this measurement.

6. From the construction, shelf, or butcher paper, cut a rectangle that measures the same from the top to bottom as the can and measures one-half inch more in length than the can measures around.

7. Wrap this paper rectangle around the can and tape or glue it where the ends overlap.

8. Turn the covered can into a creature by taping or gluing on such features as eyes, ears, a nose, a mouth, teeth, whiskers, horns, and a tail.

Bodacious Bookmarks

People who love to read will enjoy having a custom-made bookmark.

Begin by cutting strips about one and a half inches wide and six inches long from colored paper or thin cardboard.

Here are some ideas for decorating your bookmarks:

Use stickers or cancelled postage stamps to decorate a bookmark.

Use felt markers and draw bold geometric designs.

Decorate a bookmark with various colors and sizes of ribbon.

When you are finished decorating your bookmark, cover both sides with clear plastic film to make it more durable and attractive.

Punch a hole near the end of your bookmark, and add a loop of yarn or embroidery thread.

Cut out and glue magazine pictures using a theme such as flowers, cats, or birds.

Use dried flowers and grasses to decorate a bookmark. Arrange the flowers on the bookmark, and hold them in place with white glue that will dry clear.

Animal Stone Paintings

These cheerful, creative creatures make perfect gifts for kids and senior citizens.

WHAT YOU NEED

- assorted smooth stones
- old toothbrush
- bucket or bowl
- detergent
- water
- acrylic paints in assorted colors
- paintbrush
- water cup

WHAT YOU DO

1. Find some smooth stones.

2. Put detergent and hot water in a bucket or bowl.

3. Soak the stones in the hot, soapy water. Scrub the stones with the toothbrush to remove dirt and mud.

4. Rinse the stones in clean water, and allow them to dry thoroughly.

5. Study the stones from all angles. Do their shapes and textures remind you of certain animals? Does one spot stick out like a nose or tail? Do hollow, dark areas suggest eyes?

6. Paint the stones to look like colorful animals.

Closing Thoughts

Do One Kind Thing

As you go about your day,
Do one kind thing along the way.
Make a meal for those in need,
Or help a youngster learn to read.
Visit someone who's alone,
In a hospital or nursing home.
Donate blankets or plant a tree.
Try to right the wrongs you see.
Pick up litter on a beach,
Or choose a skill you'd like to teach.
Give shelter to a lonely pet,
Write to a senior you've never met.
There are lots of ways you can help,
And make your presence truly felt.
Just think of simple things to do,
That show that special side of you.
And as you go about your day,
Do one kind thing along the way.

—Linda Schwartz